TRUMP &
THE MAGA MOVEMENT
AS ANTI-CHRIST

TRUMP & THE MAGA MOVEMENT AS ANTI-CHRIST

A Handbook for the 2024 Election

Foreword by Caroline Myss

Matthew Fox

Afterword by Andrew Harvey

TRUMP & THE MAGA MOVEMENT AS ANTI-CHRIST
A HANDBOOK FOR THE 2024 ELECTION

Copyright © 2024 Matthew Fox.

All rights reserved. No part of this book may be used or reproduced by any means, graphic, electronic, or mechanical, including photocopying, recording, taping or by any information storage retrieval system without the written permission of the author except in the case of brief quotations embodied in critical articles and reviews.

iUniverse books may be ordered through booksellers or by contacting:

iUniverse
1663 Liberty Drive
Bloomington, IN 47403
www.iuniverse.com
844-349-9409

Also available in audio book at http://www.matthewfox.org

Because of the dynamic nature of the Internet, any web addresses or links contained in this book may have changed since publication and may no longer be valid. The views expressed in this work are solely those of the author and do not necessarily reflect the views of the publisher, and the publisher hereby disclaims any responsibility for them.

Any people depicted in stock imagery provided by Getty Images are models, and such images are being used for illustrative purposes only.
Certain stock imagery © Getty Images.

ISBN: 978-1-6632-6526-5 (sc)
ISBN: 978-1-6632-6527-2 (e)

Print information available on the last page.

iUniverse rev. date: 09/11/2024

I dedicate this book to the young leaders of the world. And all those who are not in denial about climate change and recognize our Earth as sacred and worth saving. And to those who believe that a government of the people, by the people and for the people is an aspiration worth struggling to preserve and improve upon. And who prefer biophilia to necrophilia, joy to grievance, love to hate, and justice to greed that guarantees injustice.

CONTENTS

Foreword by Caroline Myss xi
Introduction xv

Chapter 1   Freud's Encounter with the Antichrist
            Painting in Orvieto Cathedral................................1
Chapter 2   The Antichrist as a Naming of Evil 9
Chapter 3   Christ as Archetype.......................................13
Chapter 4   Antichrist as Archetype 23
Chapter 5   Jesus and Democracy 31
Chapter 6   MAGA: Making America Grotesque Again 51
Chapter 7   18 Signs of the Times: The Antichrist in
            American Politics, 2024..57
Chapter 8   Hildegard of Bingen: The Antichrist as Patriarchy...81

Conclusion: Be a Camel and Escape the Allurement
    of the Antichrist...85
Epilogue: Christ, Antichrist, and the 2024 Election.....................93
Afterword by Andrew Harvey 95
Appendix: MAGA's Precarious Manhood vs. Authentic
    Masculinity...99
Endnotes..105
Acknowledgements 115
About the Author 117
Books by Matthew Fox 119

Christ teaches the dignity of human nature....and the full participation in Divinity which is truly humanity's happiness and the goal of human life.

—Thomas Aquinas

The disregard of the common good is greater under an oligarchy than under a democracy, where, after all, the welfare of the majority has been attempted. But worst of all is a tyranny where the advantage of one man is sought... The rule of a tyrant is worst. Security is banished and everything is uncertain when people are cut off from law and depend on the will, I would even say the greed, of another. A tyrant oppresses the bodies of his subjects, but what is more damnable, he threatens their spiritual growth, for he is set on his own power, not their progress. He is suspicious of any dignity that they may possess that will prejudice his own iniquitous domination. A tyrant is more fearful of good persons than of bad persons, for he dreads their strange virtue. Fearful lest they grow strong and so stout of heart as no longer to brook his wicked despotism, but resolve in companionship to enjoy the fruits of peace, a tyrant is constrained to destroy good people's confidence in one another, lest they band together to throw off his yoke. Therefore, he sows discord among them, and encourages dissensions and litigation.

—Thomas Aquinas

Avarice gives rise to insensibility to compassion, because one's heart is not softened by compassion to assist the needy with one's riches... It also gives rise to restlessness, by hindering one with excessive anxiety and care, for 'an avaricious man shall not be satisfied with money' (Ecclesiastes 5:9)... The avaricious in acquiring other people's goods, sometimes employ force, which pertains to violence; sometimes deceit, and then if they have recourse to words, it is falsehood, if it be mere words; perjury if they confirm their statement by oath. If they have recourse to deeds, and the deceit affects things, we have fraud.

—Thomas Aquinas

FOREWORD

by Caroline Myss

If there was ever a time, a moment, for examining the archetype of the Antichrist, it is now.

Though most people are familiar with the word, I am certain that few have ever thought of the Antichrist as an archetypal pattern. But it is. An archetype is a pattern of power, akin to a psychic magnetic organizer, that governs the development of our psyche. Archetypes are like psychic road maps that give us an inner path of perception to follow throughout our lives.

The Antichrist is a very powerful archetype, though we should think of it as one of the grand arcana in the archetype cosmos because of its association with demonic forces that continually wage war against the Light of the Divine. That is, this archetype requires a collective psychic alchemy to emerge within society or particular groups within a society.

If there is such a force as the Antichrist, and I believe there is, I believe that animating this dark presence requires a rising collective atmosphere of fear, lawlessness, entitlement, hatred, prejudice, and panic. Combine those shadow human behaviors with growing social, political, economic and now environmental crises, which only exacerbate the fear that we cannot or will not survive the rapid changes in our world.

The Antichrist is associated with being a single male figure capable of seducing numerous people into believing a false message that mimics the message of redemption in some way, such as, "I am the one who can save you," or "I am your retribution," or "This society will fail without me," and "We are being invaded by terrorists, murderers, drug dealers all coming to destroy the life you have."

The Antichrist thrives in chaos and though he presents himself as the person best suited to calm the social waters, in truth, the Antichrist is an agent of chaos and turmoil. Indeed, the Antichrist requires that people suffer so that he can appear to be the redeemer.

Could Donald Trump be a genuine Antichrist figure, hellbent on destroying the social order of world community? Well, as writer Rick Wilson so aptly noted in his book, *Everything Trump Touches Dies*, it seems that people who get involved with him in any way end up compromising their soul, and certainly their integrity. No former cabinet member of Trump's will endorse him. Indeed, they have publicly urged people to never allow Trump near the White House again. Lawyers have lost their license to practice law as a result of working for Trump.

And numerous people are now serving time in prison because they believed his Big Lie, that the election of 2020 was stolen from him. And his Project 2025 has been exposed as an about 900-page plan to dismantle the American system of government, except for the chosen elite. No one so far as I know has ever once said, "Because of Donald Trump, I am healthier today. I am successful. I am thriving." Empowerment of others, even in the slightest way, is impossible for Donald Trump.

Jesus referred to Satan as the Father of Lies and for Jesus lying was pure evil, an act of conscious deception of others. Journalists have tracked an estimated 33,000 lies told by Trump during his four-year term as President of the United States. He is a man incapable of speaking the truth. He supports violence and is driven by vengeance. And he finds it impossible to say anything kind to anyone. None of his characteristics – and I do mean none – inspire people to treat others kindly, to be generous, to be inclusive to all living creatures, as the Dalai Lama so often directs.

Read this book with an open mind. Good and evil are real forces in our world.

INTRODUCTION

AN "AHA!" MOMENT IN A CHURCH IN ORVIETO

Recently I underwent an "Aha!" moment on visiting a church in Orvieto, Italy. I was in town to teach a week course on the Spirituality of Thomas Aquinas in honor of the 800th anniversary of his birth and 750th anniversary of his death. This particular church was a beautiful and art-filled Cathedral begun in the 13th century (shortly after Aquinas lived) and it contained a renowned painting by Luca Signorelli entitled "The Antichrist." I reproduce that painting on the cover and inside of this book (see pages 38-41 below). Accompanying me in the church was my Italian friend Gianluigi Gugliermetto (GG) a fellow Episcopal priest who did his theological studies at Claremont University in California and has translated a number of my books into Italian. Indeed, part of my trip to Italy was to give two talks on the most recent book he has translated, that on *The Reinvention of Work.* (Which they called in Italian, *Work as Life.*)

The "Aha!" moment occurred when Gianluigi and I were looking at the giant painting entitled the "Antichrist" which covered an entire wall in a large chapel within the Cathedral of the Assumption. Painted at the very beginning of the sixteenth century, it inspired Michelangelo and other painters.

My first response on looking at the large fresco on the left wall on the Antichrist came from my gut, not my head. On viewing it, I said out loud: "It feels like Donald Trump." The principal figure was preaching to a sizeable crowd of people, a number of whom were in rapt attention. He had sort of a hair problem as his hair stood up in two places and resembled horns. There was a demon whispering in his ear telling him what to say.

As one looked more carefully at the crowd in the painting, one saw a number of people who had been beaten up by persons listening to this preacher. There was violence and hostility afoot in the crowd. There were some groups of people set off from the crowd arguing with one another and apparently disagreeing with the speaker and in the back, there were what one person calls "ninja-like figures" dressed in all black outfits spread out on the steps of a huge church that left an impression of darkness and menace. Indeed, Nicholas Fox Weber compares the men in black outfits "dancing their hideous dance" to the Ku Klux Klan.

Until I saw that painting in Orvieto I had always shied away from speaking about the "Antichrist." I felt that kind of apocalyptic language was owned too much by fundamentalist ideologues and was too subject to manipulation.

However, given the realities of today's Armageddon-like atmosphere with many nations reverting to fascist ways in their politics and elevating leaders who are outspoken radical right revolutionaries; and with powerful corporations such as the Koch brothers, the Heritage Foundation, Opus Dei and others striving mightily to end democracy as we know it; and with white supremacism on the rise and so-called "Christian nationalism" represented in very high places; and a now completely compromised unsupreme court; and the fascist "Project 2025" being offered as a blueprint for a second Trumpian presidency, I am struck anew by the power of the Antichrist archetype.

What is clear from this rich painting with 156 different characters in it by my count is what a *contemporary twist the painter put on the archetype of the Antichrist.* Instead of conceiving of the Antichrist as a future event, he pictures his presence in his own day amidst both ordinary and famous people—Christopher Columbus, Dante and the artist himself all play a role in this fresco. The artist is pictured in the left-hand corner observing the theatrical scene alongside esteemed artist Fra Angelico who also contributed paintings in the chapel. It has been suggested also that the artist and the Antichrist share the same visage.

This gives us permission to speak of the Antichrist in the context of today's political and moral landscape—which is what my intention is in offering this book as a commentary on the news of our day.

Many pundits have observed how the Republican party under Trump has become less a party than a "cult." But they have not specified what kind of cult it is. In this book I raise the question: It this cult a 21st century version of a Cult of the Antichrist?

The Antichrist is a symbol found in apocalyptic literature of the Bible and has often appeared in Christian history such as in the powerful painting by Signorelli in the Orvieto Cathedral in the early 16th century—a painting that "bowled over" Sigmund Freud and was "like a bomb" in his life (see chapter one). Many others have been similarly struck by the painting, including myself. We explore its meaning vis-à-vis evil in chapter two. And its opposite, Christ, in chapter three. And its fuller meaning as archetype in chapter four. And we consider how Jesus, as 14th century mystic and prophet Meister Eckhart interprets him, was a precursor of democracy (chapter five). In chapter six we address what may be a deeper meaning to the acronym MAGA and in chapter seven we name 18 elements of the Antichrist in American politics today. (18 is the summary number of 666, a number associated with the Antichrist.) In chapter eight we consider the paintings and teachings of 12th century abbess, saint and doctor of the church, Hildegard of Bingen, who connects the archetype directly to patriarchy. In the Conclusion we offer practical advice on arming oneself and society against succumbing to allurements of the Antichrist aura and mystique. We share ten pictures in the center of this book, two painted by Hildegard—one of Christ and another of the Antichrist; and 8 from the frescoes by Fra Angelico and Luca Signorelli. The cover is a closeup from Signorelli's Antichrist painting.

This is my third book on Evil. My first, *Sins of the Spirit, Blessings of the Flesh: Transforming Evil in Soul and Society*, sought to develop a new language for talking about evil by relating the wisdom of the East with the wisdom of the West on the topic. The second, *The Pope's War: How Ratzinger's Secret Crusade Has Imperiled the Church and How It Can Be Saved*, took a hard look at evil in institutional religion and culture through two papacies in my lifetime. And now this, that looks at evil through the archetype of the Antichrist with the help of artists such as Hildegard of Bingen and Luca Signorelli and the author of the Book of Revelation.

Recall that not only did Hildegard and Signorelli employ the language of the Antichrist, but Martin Luther did so from the year 1520 to his death 25 years later. After studying Lorenzo Valla's denunciation of the alleged Donation of Constantine as a forgery in 1520, Luther applied the trope first to the curia and then to the pope. He cited Matthew 24: 2, Thessalonians 2:9, Daniel 2, 7, 8, 9 and the Book of Revelation chapters 13, 14, 17 and 18 in making his case. Eventually other reformers including Zwingli, Calvin, Knox and Cramner applied the Antichrist symbol to the papacy of their day as well. So applying the Antichrist archetype as we do in this book to Trump and the MAGA world and its values is not at all without precedent.

Any discussion of evil must be wrapped in a larger context understood as an Original Blessing, to seeing the history of the universe for what it is: An unfathomable gift and mystery of goodness and grace that has brought us forward along with countless other species and galaxies and planets. That we wrestle with evil is integral to our existence. But existence itself remains an ineffable mystery evoking ongoing beauty, wonder, awe—and one hopes--gratitude in return.

CHAPTER ONE

FREUD'S ENCOUNTER WITH THE ANTICHRIST PAINTING IN ORVIETO CATHEDRAL

Curiously, the paintings in the Orvieto Cathedral enticed Sigmund Freud so deeply that he called them "the finest paintings I have ever seen." In his book, *Freud's Trip to Orvieto,* art historian Nicholas Weber tells us that good art was "mind-altering" for Freud and affected him "viscerally," so his judgment on Signorelli's paintings are "a fact of inestimable significance." Freud visited Orvieto three times, the first time was in 1897 shortly after his father died. He returned in 1902 and 1907. That he actually left the city of Vienna three times to travel to Orvieto (a town of only 20,000 people today though it was 30,000 persons in the Middle Ages) to study the paintings in greater depth raises the question: "Why would Freud want to do that?"

His experience of the chapel with the frescoes has been called a "bomb" to Freud's psyche and some have suggested his theory of psychoanalysis was born there as a result. Freud's letters from Orvieto in his first trip contain the first reference to his theory of the psyche and at least one biographer says that the shock of seeing good and evil, Eros and Thanatos, depicted so vividly on the opposite walls of the chapel created a turmoil in him from which his whole vision of the human being emerged. The evil of the fresco of the Antichrist with all the falsehood, the paramilitary troops, the violence, is contrasted on the other wall with the vision of the resurrection of the flesh, friendship and love. That wall also contains a dynamic and "grizzly" picture of hell. Both love and beauty as well as death and hell are present to humanity, both are real options.

Freud's encounter with what Weber calls "Signorelli's masterpiece" became "one of the most significant pilgrimages of his life" and it would "make a profound mark on his work." One result was his theory of repressed memories since a few years later, while talking with an acquaintance on a train ride, he was not able to recall the name of the painter, Signorelli, of this favorite painting of his. "Inner torment" ensued, according to Freud, and it concerned him so much that five days later he wrote an essay on "The Phenomenon of Forgetfulness" and in 1901 he opens his book, *The Psychopathology of Everyday Life,* with a discussion of his inability to recall Signorelli's name and the "repressed thoughts" therein. So it was clearly an issue for him. Wrestling with that problem, Freud concluded that his stumbling was due to a "repressed memory."

The "New Chapel" or "Chapel of Saint Britius" which housed Signorelli's frescoes was built in the first half of the 15th century. The frescoes on the three walls have been called "one of the highest examples of Italian painting." Esteemed Dominican friar Fra Angelico was the first artist hired to decorate the walls of this chapel in 1447. He completed only two paintings, however, that of "Christ the Judge" and "Angels and Prophets" before he was called back to Rome by Pope Nicolas V for other work. It was fifty years later, in 1499, that Luca Signorelli was hired to finish the chapel and he chose to depict the great cycle of the Last Judgement. On the left wall is "Rule of the Antichrist" and on the right wall are "The Resurrection of the Flesh" and "Hell." It is said that Michelangelo sought inspiration from this painting and stayed three months in Orvieto to study these paintings and especially the one on hell.

By the time Signorelli was hired to finish the work, people were focusing on the meaning of the year 1500. "With the world entering a new half millennium many saw an apocalypse coming. The subject matter long familiar to Christian iconography now has a new immediacy." That subject being of course the Last Judgement. Jungian scholar Edward Edinger, in his major study on the Apocalypse, sees the apocalypse archetype "constellating very powerfully" also in our time, both in the individual and the collective. He understands the "apocalypse" psychologically to mean "the momentous event of the coming of the Self into conscious realization." Whether in the individual psyche or the collective group, "in either case it is a momentous event—literally world-shattering. This is what the content of the Apocalypse archetype presents: the shattering of the world as it has been, followed by its reconstitution." The breakdown of social structures whether political, ethnic or religious, accompany such an event.

Freud was not a Christian of course and was a Jew but not a practicing one. In fact, he called himself an atheist and his basic attitude toward religion was not particularly positive or affirming. He recognized how his Jewish heritage played an important role in the development of his thought and his identity and took a keen interest in religion. He was well aware of the antisemitism that permeated Germany and Austria in his time and wrote in 1925 that "I prefer to call myself a Jew" rather than a German for that very reason.

Freud proposed that religion is an "illusion" and a neurosis and possibly an attempt to gain control over the external world. Maybe it was an attempt to control the Oedipal complex. He wrote at least four books about religion. Among them were *Totem and Taboo* (1913); *The Future of an Illusion* (1927); *Civilization and Its Discontents* (1930); and *Moses and Monotheism* (1939). In 1933, in his "New Introductory Lectures on Psychoanalysis," Freud wrote: "Religion is an illusion, and it derives its strength from its readiness to fit in with our instinctual wishful impulses." He goes on: "If we attempt to assign the place of religion in the evolution of making it appears not as a permanent acquisition but as a counterpart to the neurosis which individual civilized men have to go through in their passage from childhood to maturity." In *The Future of an Illusion,*" he wrote that "religion is comparable to a childhood neurosis." He refers to religious teaching as "neurotic relics" that need to be replaced through the "rational operation of the intellect."

And in *Civilization and Its Discontents* Freud declares that "the whole thing is so patently infantile, so foreign to reality, that to anyone with a friendly attitude to humanity it is painful to think that the great majority of mortals will never be able to rise above this view of life." He saw the sense of sin or guilt to have played a large role in civilization and in religion.

Psychologically, he saw religion as the unconscious mind's need for wish fulfillment and people who believe in God do so because he represents a powerful father figure, and they need to feel secure and absolve themselves of guilt.

Given all this disparaging of religion from Freud, it is all the more curious why he—of all people—would choose to uproot himself from Vienna on several occasions and visit a small town in Italy and park himself inside a Christian Cathedral to study paintings about the Antichrist, heaven and hell.

Freud was still in the early days of his own self-analysis when he first arrived in Orvieto which proved to be "one of the significant pilgrimages of his life. It would also make its mark on his work…" Nicholas Fox Weber, in his extraordinary book called *Freud's Trip to Orvieto: The Great Doctor's Unresolved Confrontation with Antisemitism, Death, and Homoeroticism; His Passion for Paintings; and the Writer in His Footsteps*, explores in depth the reasons why Freud repressed the name of this artist of his favorite painting. He points out how the encounter with the Antichrist painting awakened his own oppression as a Jew since Jews have often been depicted as "Antichrist." Freud held "his own ambivalence about being Jewish" and in Signorelli's world, "to be Jewish was to side with the devil and to be destined for hell." Antisemitism was rampant in 1897 when Freud saw the paintings as well as in 1500 when Signorelli was painting them and the Spanish Inquisition was at its peak.

In Freud's Vienna, Karl Lueger, a "notorious antisemite" had just been elected mayor for the third time. Called "a forerunner of Hitler," he based his entire political philosophy on the persecution of the Jews. He halted Jews from being on the University of Vienna faculty and thus prevented Freud from becoming a full professor there. Antisemitism also triggered an issue Freud had with his father—who had recently died—regarding his meekness when it came to standing up to antisemites.

And it also echoed his attraction—even as a boy—to male hero types such as Hannibal since so many of the men in Signorelli's paintings are, in Weber's words, "testosterone itself." Weber summarizes his observations this way: Freud had to avoid a side of himself that was "too painful to bear" in the presence of Signorelli's frescoes. The longing, perhaps, to be more like the "mighty males who proliferate in the frescoes; his admiration for their bodies and physical strength; the wish for his father to have had their power... his worries about the connection of Jewishness and maleness—all of it was so overwhelming, even to the most probing of minds." Thus does Weber summarize his understanding of the impact that Signorelli's frescoes had on Freud.

Weber's book has been called an "unusual meditation on sex, death, art, and Jewishness." One element of the frescoes that shook Freud up to the point that he repressed the artist's name was "his reaction to the work's homoerotism." This is especially apparent in his murals on The Resurrection of the Flesh and on Hell which Weber describes as "a vivid depiction of muscular nude men...burly specimens of raw masculine powers...with their ripped torsos and gladiators' limbs, they go to the limits of their physical force."

Weber had his own powerful response to the frescoes. "Signorelli's frescoes, which narrate the end of the world, were unlike anything I had ever seen... The colors terrify us. The amount of death and violence is destabilizing. This is both the end of life and the start of a miserable afterlife... The powerful connection between sexuality, punishment, and death in this violent world of musclemen leaves the viewer whirling... The artwork alone struck me as ample reason for a memory loss... There was a lot in Signorelli's frescoes that would want to make one cover one's eyes or turn away." No wonder Freud was driven to forget parts of these paintings.

According to Weber, the issues that Freud faced with these paintings at Orvieto were: "strength versus weakness, his sense of himself in relation to his father, and the connection between death and sexuality, the ultimate aliveness." Two subjects that most "obsessed Freud" were "masculinity and Judaism." And both are center stage with these frescoes which depict, according to Weber, "raw masculinity."

Demons had a certain attraction to Freud who tells the story of how, when he was a young man living in Paris, "the platform for Notre Dame was my favorite resort in Paris; every free afternoon I used to clamber about there on the towers of the church between the monsters and the devils." Weber adds, "demons, as they were conceived and depicted in Christian eyes, attracted Freud like magnets." There are no shortage of monsters and demons in Signorelli's chapel.

Freud encountering Signorelli's frescoes the year he did was a pivotal event for him. He was undergoing the Jewish year of mourning of his father's death as well as his own self-analysis and was "fine-tuning" his views on the Oedipus complex and origins of hysteria that very year. He said that a man losing one's father constitutes "the most important event, the most poignant loss, of a man's life." And he was trying to forget the suicide of one of his patients when he was on that train ride where he forgot Signorelli's name.

CHAPTER TWO

THE ANTICHRIST AS A NAMING OF EVIL

As I have had more time to meditate on the painting and its meaning, I think I have the answer to my question why Freud was so taken by it. It lies in the nature of the "Antichrist" archetype itself. The Antichrist archetype stands for evil. It therefore raises questions in all of us of our participation and complicity, our guilt or freedom from guilt, in works of evil. Surely that was at the heart of Freud's keen interest in that particular painting. As it is mine in writing this short book about the presidential election of 2024.

In what way are we complicit—or choosing not to be—in the destruction of democracy and the 248-year experiment in it carried on by our American ancestors? That question seems to be at the heart of the history we are living through—as well as making-- at this moment in time.

Talking about evil is never easy—especially for Americans because many people came here escaping traumas of their past whether poverty or famine or wars or prejudice and they did not want to dwell on their past but look ahead to creating new possibilities. And also, it is not easy because much of the foundation of America was at the expense of slavery which meant bringing over ten million people here against their will. A calamitous civil war proved necessary to purge America of that evil--yet that did not altogether succeed. Not long after passing constitutional amendments to insure equality following the war, union soldiers were withdrawn from the southern states and Jim Crow laws and lynchings and voting obstructions flourished with the purpose of continuing to subjugate black people. Brown vs Board of Education and the marches and beatings and jailings that began in the 1950s and brought about civil rights legislation in the 1960s represented a giant step forward, but even those gains have been seriously diminished thanks to congressional inaction and Supreme Court actions in the past thirty years. So the struggle against the evils of racism continue.

Another evil upon which America was built is the dispossessing of the indigenous people of their original lands. This has resulted in many years of inherited trauma and outright thievery against the original inhabitants of this land and that too is very difficult for Americans to talk about.

Another reason why evil is hard to talk about is that religion has often distorted the topic by overselling guilt and "sin." Sin itself can easily be reduced to trivia and when religion defines itself almost exclusively as redemption, it leaves out the deeper dimensions to religion such as gratitude and joy and celebration that are our response to being alive and part of creation and community. As well as the co-creative work for justice and the common good and compassion that preserves that creation. Sin is a much smaller concept than evil.

In an attempt to correct the reductionism on evil, I wrote a major study on the subject eight years ago wherein I offered a new language by which to talk about evil, one that bypassed the sin-dominated mind set. I did this by marrying language from the East in conjunction with language from the West, showing how the 7 chakras of the East complement the 7 capital sins of the West. Aquinas defines sin as "misdirected love," but the chakras name seven areas of love in our psyches and bodies, thus sin would be equivalent to an off-center chakra. (The Hebrew word for sin is an archery term meaning to miss the bullseye).

I also moved off the negative connotations of the word "flesh" that seems to over dominate religious discussions about evil and incorporate this dimension in the title of my book. Aquinas dared to say that "sins of the spirit are far more grave than sins of the flesh" because the latter takes one toward God, but the former takes one away from God. Thus, the title of my book, *Sins of the Spirit, Blessings of the Flesh: Transforming Evil in Soul and Society*.

Today's science has linked up with the non-dualistic tradition in healthy religion by reminding us that all matter is flesh and all matter is light, thus we can erase forever the dualism of spirit vs. matter and redeem the word "flesh." Thus I offer in my book three chapters on recovering the wonders and sacredness to be found in 1) the flesh of the universe and 2) the flesh of the earth and 3) the flesh of the human body (and other bodies on earth).

Since it is not easy to talk about evil and my development of an alternative language took 450 pages in my book, I welcome the brevity of an archetype such as "Antichrist" that can capture the sense of the word "evil" so succinctly. And that, because it is not a rational term in itself, strikes one at a deeper level than the rational brain alone. There is a kind of intuitive or "gut" response to the term "Antichrist" as there was to my encounter with the painting by the same name by Signorelli. One feels in it some of the depth and pungency that accompanies the word "evil." Certainly Freud felt it.

CHAPTER THREE

CHRIST AS ARCHETYPE

To understand a metaphor or archetype of the "Antichrist" we would have to begin by considering Christ. For the former emerges clearly in response to the latter. *The "Antichrist" stands for the polar opposite of Christ.*

And who, what is Christ? Christ stands for the Good, the merciful, the compassionate, the just, the godly. And it can operate as a projection for all these realities. Christ stands for the best in ourselves and in all beings. In other words, for the image and likeness of the divine that all beings carry within us. Nancy Abrams has written a book about how we can talk about God today and she concludes that the best contemporary name for God is, "Aspiration."

Christ is a term that stands for "aspiration." The best of ourselves therefore. *Tselem* is the Jewish word for image of God and rabbi David Seidenberg, in his impressive study on *Kabbalah and Ecology,* has determined that the Jewish tradition teaches that all beings carry this divine element in themselves. The mystical tradition in Judaism and in Islam (Avicenna for example and Rumi too) and in Christianity (Meister Eckhart in particular) call it "the spark of God" that is in all things.

Christ stands for the Truth also. We aspire to the truth. "I am the way and the truth" is a well-known statement in John's Gospel. Whether it is the historical Jesus talking or the Cosmic Christ, words put into Jesus' mouth by those who knew him or came after him, is slightly irrelevant. That his followers saw him as standing for Truth is what most matters. It is aspirational. Truth is one of the most universal names for the divine world over.

And Christ also stands for the Light. "I am the light of the world" (Jn 8:12) and "do not hide your light under a basket but put it on a stool so all can see it" (Mt 5:15). This readily connects to his Jewish heritage. In the Jewish tradition we learn that light was the first thing created by the Creator who said, "Let there be light," and there was light. "God saw that light was good, and God divided light from darkness. God called light 'day' and darkness he called 'night'" (Gen 1:5).

In Psalm 104, a creation story older than Genesis chapter 1, the psalmist sings how Divinity itself comes robed in light: "Yahweh my God, how great you are! Clothed in majesty and glory, wrapped in a robe of light!" (Ps 104:1f). The word "glory" bespeaks light, radiance, and splendor and God is called the "king of glory" who has poured out the divine radiance into creation. "The heavens declare the glory of God, and the firmament proclaims His handwork" (Ps 19:1).

The great mystical work in Judaism is called *Zohar* which means *radiance, splendor, brilliance*. According to the *Zohar*, creation began as a "blinding spark."

> "Sparks burst into flashes, up high and down below
> then quieted down and rose up high, beyond, beyond....
> The spark expanded, whirling around and round."

According to the *Kabbalah*, another Jewish mystical work, one elevates physical desire to spiritual desire by drawing out the "holy spark" that dwells within. "You bring forth holy sparks from the natural world. There is no path greater than this. For wherever you go and whatever you do—even mundane activities—you serve God."

Wisdom in the Jewish Bible is called "a reflection of light, a spotless mirror of the working of God," and "an image of his goodness." In the Gospels, Jesus is presented as Wisdom incarnate, wisdom made flesh among us and having entered history. In John's Gospel we are told that "the Word was the true light that enlightened all people; and he was coming into the world" (Jn 1:9). And Christ is reported to say: "As long as I am in the world, I am the light of the world" (Jn 9:5). And again, "all that came to be had life in him and that life was the light of people, a light that shines in the dark, a light that darkness could not overcome" (Jn 1:4f).

In the Gospel of Thomas, Jesus says, "If they say to you: 'Where are you from?' say to them: 'We came from the light there, where the light was, by itself. It stood boldly and manifested itself in their image.'"

Paul calls the risen Christ "the Lord of glory" and says that "we all, with faces unveiled, reflecting as in a mirror the glory of the Lord, are being transformed into His very image from glory to glory, as through the Spirit of the Lord" (2 Cor: 3:18). All of us incarnate the light of Christ therefore and are invited to be other Christs.

Christian mystics celebrate Christ as light in all creation and in us. Hildegard of Bingen said:

> "I, the fiery life of divine wisdom,
> I ignite the beauty of the plains,
> I sparkle the waters,
> I burn in the sun, and the moon, and the stars."

She calls God the fire in all things. "God says: 'I am the supreme fire; not deadly, but rather enkindling every spark of life.'"

She asks:

> "Who is the Holy Spirit?
> The Holy Spirit is a Burning Spirit.
> It kindles the hearts of humankind.
> Like tympanum and lyre it plays them,
> gathering volume in the temple of the soul."

She called her paintings of her visions and meditations "illuminations."

Mechtild of Magdeburg, a Beguine and member of the women's movement of the thirteenth century, says: "Lie down in the Fire. See and taste the flowing Godhead through your being. Feel the Holy Spirit moving and compelling you within the flowing Fire and Light of God."

Meister Eckhart says that "something like a brilliant light that glows incessantly and something like a burning fire which burns incessantly" happens inside of us. This is the "spark of the soul" and "this fire is nothing other than the Holy Spirit, a divine light, a ray, an imprinted picture of the divine nature."

Thomas Aquinas says, "God is light; and one who approaches this light is illuminated, as Isaiah says: 'Rise, in love, and be enlightened.'" Aquinas recognizes a divine radiance to be found in every creature. "God puts into creatures, along with a kind of 'sheen,' a reflection of God's own luminous 'ray,' which is the fountain of all light... Shining reflections of the divine radiance must be understood as the sharing of God's likeness and constitute those beautifying reflections that make beauty in things." Sounding a lot like post-Einsteinian science, Aquinas says that "the being of things is itself their light and the measure of the being of a thing is the measure of its light."

Today's science is telling us that there are photons or light waves in every atom in the universe. This seems to put meat on the bones of Christ being called the "light in all things" in John 1. Physicist David Bohm declares that matter is "frozen light" or very slow-moving light, thus eliminating forever the dualism between matter and spirit (since so many spiritual traditions world over equate divinity and light). Einstein confessed that he wanted to devote his entire life to studying light.

The theme of connecting Light and Divinity is found all around the world and among all world religions. In Africa or Egypt, called Kemet, the Creator was honored for bringing forth light.

> "Primeval without equal,
> Creator of men and gods,
> Living flame that came from Num,
> Maker of light for mankind."

Celtic scholar John O'Donohue tells us that "the Celtic mind adored the light… Ultimately, light is the mother of life. Where there is no light, there can be no life… Light is the secret presence of the divine. It keeps life awake." The ancient poet who created the prayer called "The Deer's Cry" attributes his rising every morning to Light:

> "Strength of heaven,
> Light of sun,
> Radiance of moon,
> Splendor of fire."

A Gaelic poem venerates the sun as the eye and face of God.

> "The eye of the great God,
> The eye of the God of glory,
> ...pouring upon us at each time and season...
> Glory to thee
> Thou glorious sun.
> Glory to thee, thou sun,
> Face of the God of life."

The *Bhagavad Gita* celebrates the divine origin of light. Krishna, the supreme Godhead speaks: "The splendor of the sun, which dissipates the darkness of this whole world, comes from Me. And the splendor of the moon and the splendor of fire are also from Me."

We are told that "Krishna is the source of light in all luminous objects. He is beyond the darkness of matter and is unmanifested.... He is situated in everyone's heart."

In the *Vedas* we hear Brahman declare:

> "The cosmic waters glow. I am Light!
> The light glows. I am Brahman!"

Atman is a great light residing inside of us. "There is a Light that shines above this heaven, above all worlds, above everything that exists in the highest worlds beyond which there are no higher—this is the Light that shines within humans."

What and Who is Christ? We have said that Christ is the projection of the best of ourselves. Our best *aspirations of who we might become.* This includes our capacity for compassion and caring, for putting justice ahead of greed and injustice that greed spawns. Our capacity for forgiveness rather than revenge and hatred and rage against others whom we label our "enemies." Jesus tells us we are all capable of such powers. The best of ourselves includes therefore our divinity, our share in the grace of divine love that has birthed this universe and continues to birth it—even through us and our work and decisions and choices we make. The divine gets incarnated in us as it got incarnated in Jesus and the archetype of Christ helps name that entering of history and taking on matter and flesh in time for us. Our being other Christs and true "sons and daughters" of God. It names our being linked in a deep way with the on-going unfolding of this amazing universe of 13.8 billion years in time and of two trillion galaxies in space, each with billions of stars within them.

Being "sons and daughters of God," other Christs (or Buddhas or Images of God), we are wisdom keepers and sons and daughters of Wisdom. Yes, wisdom becomes incarnate in us as in Jesus and the Christ. Our aspiration too is to become wisdom incarnate. Thus, other Christs.

I recall a conversation with a rabbi many years ago who said to me, "in our tradition, anyone who is living a life of wisdom is rightly called a "son or daughter of God" and since I consider Jesus to have been a liver and teacher of wisdom, I have no problem at all calling him 'a Son of God.'" What this rabbi said of Jesus can be said of him and, hopefully, of all of us. At least that is our aspiration. And Jesus planted that aspiration in very ordinary persons whom he called to follow him including but not limited to fishermen like Peter and others, tax collectors like Matthew, healers like Mary Magdalene and Luke, peasant farmers like his brother James and rabbis like Paul.

Christ is God become human in time and history in the person of Jesus but also in all of us. When Eckhart asks at a Christmas Liturgy, "What good is it to me if Mary gave birth to the Son of God and I do not do the same?" he is carrying on this same understanding of the omnipresence of Christ in time and history. The Christ event was not a one-off event. It is still going on—or ought to be—this incarnating of the divine in ourselves, imperfect instruments that we be. "This is the fullness of time, when the Son of God is begotten in you," Eckhart teaches. Furthermore, "God is never content unless he begets his Son in us." Indeed, "The son is constantly born and constantly reborn and will continually be born in God." Theologian M.D. Chenu talks of "continuous incarnation." God is always needing to be born.

All this is what it means to talk of Christ or the Christ or Jesus the Christ or the Cosmic Christ, the light in everything in the universe, humans included. Are we "the light of the world?" Are we light to one another? Are we light to ourselves? Can we find the light inside? Even amidst the limits and the shadows and the darkness? Leonard Cohen sings of the "cracks in everything" through which "the light gets in." We need not dwell exclusively on the cracks, the imperfections, but even when we do we learn that "this is how the light gets in." Light is everywhere and in all of us. That is what the presence of Christ means.

Jesus was an excellent demonstration of this in his personhood and stories and teachings and relationships. This is why he said to ordinary folk, "Come follow me." And "take up your cross" and follow me. The journey is not superficial, it is weighty and heavy and often uncomfortable. But it is real and the birthing of the Christ in us does not happen only in one expression. It happens in joy and delight as well as in emptiness and suffering and loss;

in creativity itself and in transformation of self and society and in solidarity with others.

Jesus reminds us of our potential and our capacity to dig deep into our best to ask what we have to contribute and what we are learning about life and its demands and how we can contribute and bring light to the "cracks in everything." Personal cracks and societal cracks abound. But we are here in this historical moment and can bring our own light to the occasion, ourselves to the history unfolding before us. Drawing from our deepest selves, we can bring Light and Truth into the world to combat evil and darkness and untruths. We can choose to bring the Good and the Sacred to bear on evil and suffering. The Sacred is always that which is bigger than ourselves—this is why Awe is a way we name having an experiences of the Sacred and why it is said that "awe is the beginning of wisdom." Wisdom-bearers must be struck by Awe and carriers of awe and the Sacred and that which is bigger than ourselves.

We have discussed some meanings of Christ as archetype. To summarize briefly, Christ as Light, as Truth, as Wisdom, as aspiration of the best part of ourselves that we desire to give birth to, as the "spark of the soul" that inspires us, as our better selves, as incarnated in Jesus but also in all of us and in the world's religions which honor light as divinity and divinity as light. Christ as Justice and Compassion and Forgiveness and Love and the solidarity that all humans share whether we acknowledge it or not. Christ as the son or daughter of God that is all people. And Christ as a precursor of democracy.

In the twelfth century, Hildegard of Bingen, Benedictine abbess and musical genius, author of ten books on science and theology and human nature and morality, healer and prophet who challenged popes and emperors and abbots and bishops, painted a vision of Christ. Christ as a "man in sapphire blue," the healing Christ found in all humans. In my book on recovering authentic masculinity, I offer the "Blue Man" archetype as one of the paths forward. I include Hildegard's painting in this current book.

In her painting (reproduced in this book on page 49) Hildegard offers us a veritable study of compassion. The Christ has hands extended because the power of the heart is pictured as infusing the work of his hands. This is what compassion does: it extends our heart of caring and of healing into our hands. Compassion goes to work to assist others. As Hildegard puts it, "to be foolish is to lack motherly compassion. Whoever lacks this dies of thirst." Blue, the color of water as well as of peace, is a dominant color in her image of Christ as compassion. "When you compassionately touch and cleanse the wounds of others, then I, Love, am reclining on your bed. And when you meet simple, honest people with good will and in a godly way, then I am united to you in loving friendship." Compassion is active for Hildegard, and it binds the universe and the ailing human body. It cleanses, supports, celebrates. Compassion affects us this way: "I am flooded through with inner compassion; nothing—neither gold nor money, costly stones nor pearls—can hide from me the eyes of the poor who weep because they lack life's necessities."

Now that we have considered Christ as an archetype, we are prepared to consider the Antichrist, the opposite of Christ, the incarnation of evil.

CHAPTER FOUR

ANTICHRIST AS ARCHETYPE

What is an archetype? It is a symbol which speaks universally to all humans. It can grab us like a lightning bolt and seize us from a very deep place. In the case of the Antichrist, as we have pointed out, it is a way of talking about Evil—a person or persons who preach the opposite message of that of Christ. Jungian analyst Stephen Herrmann tells us that according to Jung, "Christ is the nearest analogy to the Self in the West concerning its ultimate meaning as the Light side of God incarnated in Lord Jesus, while the other half of the Self is appearing in the archetype of Antichrist, its Dark half." The danger of a negative archetype is highlighted by Jungian scholar Edward Edinger who warns that "archetypes live themselves out in whatever psychic stuff they can appropriate, they are like devouring mouths—finding little egos they can consume, and the living out of those egos."

Carl Jung says that archetypes return when we need them. I think, in the throes of today's politics, with democracy being challenged from within, it is apparent why the Antichrist archetype has returned. When insurrectionists are cheered on by a sitting president on January 6 to attack the Capitol of the nation where Congress is gathered to practice a ritual of counting electoral votes to ensure a peaceful transfer of power, such work is the work of Antichrist forces.

In Luca Signorelli's painting of "The Preaching of the Antichrist" (reproduced in this book on pages 38-39) we behold an Antichrist that looks a lot like Christ—one's first impression is that it is Christ talking on a pedestal. That was my first impression for sure. But then things seem just a little bit weird and out of whack when one focuses more carefully on the painting. First of all, his hair is strange. It has two protrusions at the top of his head that appear horn-like. Next, there is a demonic figure whispering in his ear and they are joined together at the left arm. Furthermore, while the preacher has drawn a good-sized crowd, not all are attentive to him and in the crowd, and there is violence going on. Indeed, some persons are wounded, and some appear dead on the ground.

There are women, children, corrupt men, prostitutes, poets, rich, poor — all considering the promises the Antichrist offers. The Antichrist extends his hands for bribery money being offered to him. Piled in front of the podium is treasures the rich offer in support of the rise of the Antichrist.

Assassins are present who beat and kill those who will not bow to the false Messiah. Signorelli represents prominent figures of his day in the throng listening to this suspect messiah. Immediately on the right of the Antichrist is an old man in a yellow garment with a white collar. That is Christopher Columbus. There is a merchant paying money to a woman and a profile of Raphael and of Caesar Borgia, the son of Pope Alexandre VI who is curly haired and with a blond beard. It is said that the infamous Alexander VI "could be considered the most perfect model for antichrist…

living a secular and immoral life, indulging in indecent orgies." The pope's illegitimate son Cesare Borgia was appointed by him to be "Protector of Orvieto" and was a suspect in many unsolved murders.

Freud called the frescoes "powerful," but Weber suggests that "their power lies mainly in an increase in anxiety in the viewer." There are nobles from the family that funded the chapel and Dante Alighieri is pictured in the crowd as well.

According to one expert, "The tyrant points to his own head, signifying that only what he thinks and decides and pronounces will be the law and doctrine of the age." This seems like a clear statement about narcissism. He is in the thralls of himself, and his followers are in the thralls of him and his narcissism.

In the big questions of good and evil that the Antichrist proposes, "everyone will have to decide which side to take." The faux imitator of Christ—called the "great ape" by the church — will bring confusion to minds and hearts. "For false messiahs and false prophets will perform signs and wonders to deceive, if possible, even the elect" (Mk 13:21). "He will be a crowd-pleaser and will be worshipped like an idol." He will proclaim himself the benefactor and savior of the people and his bare feet signify poverty or trust of the poor—but beware. He is not a truth-teller. "In reality he is nothing other than a master of deceit, a lover of power, skilled in corruption, and driven by an insatiable ambition to stand above all." The image on the podium of the Antichrist is a rider on a rearing horse: a symbol of boundless pride and a prophecy of a disastrous fall. (See Rev. 20:20).

Those who allow themselves to be seduced and deceived by his words "will end up exchanging good for evil and evil for good, becoming lovers of pleasures and greedy for money, corrupt and immoral, and finally violent and homicidal... This is the totalitarian society of the Antichrist. Wicked men uniting to usurp the throne of God."

Behind the false messiah is a "small remnant" of people who will resist being confused by the Antichrist. Dominicans, Franciscans and Carmelites are resisting his teachings and seeking wisdom and truth and wanting to serve the "true Savior." From a podium in front of the Temple, the Antichrist orders the death sentence on Enoch and Elijah, two Jewish prophets who have come down from the heavenly Paradise to refute the heretical lies of the false Messiah. For their resistance, they will suffer martyrdom.

Drama is everywhere. Archangel Michael will defeat the Antichrist (Rev. 12:7f) and "the two will face each other in the greatest duel between good and evil in the history of salvation (see Rev. 18:1-3)." With mighty strength and powers, the angel of God—who is Christ himself—will defeat the usurper, casting him down head over heels into the midst of his followers, who, struck by a rain of fire, fall to the ground... Christ in his first coming casts Satan from heaven to earth, now the Angel of God will cast him into hell.

This is how the End Times conclude, and how the reign of the Antichrist ends, a reign of lies and injustice, of vanity and violence (Rev. 18:1). The usurper Antichrist has lost his place on center stage and is released to a deserted and solitary place (see Is. 14:12-15).

Behind the Antichrist and in the background a great temple is being ransacked by the followers of the Antichrist who someone described as "ninjas." The temple depicted is a picture of the original draft of St. Peter's Basilica in the Vatican. There is also a figure raised from the dead by the Antichrist who demonstrates considerable powers. It is clear that the Antichrist is not without talent and appeal. Trump too is not without talent. Thomas Aquinas astutely observed that "a politician must know more about the human soul than a doctor knows about the human body." Hitler knew the soul of his German people and appealed to its sense of resentment and grievance in Germany in the 1930's. Trump communicates with his followers in a way they find very alluring. The background landscape in Signorelli's painting is lifeless and without color and speaks to me of the devastation that wildfires are creating in our time due to climate change. The archetype of the Antichrist strikes me as a very apt symbol for our troubling times, our venture into a collective Dark Night of our Species.

In a painting he called "The Deposition," Signorelli makes a statement about death that was deeply personal for him as he interrupted his fresco project for a while to return home when his son died.

Leanne Ogasawara summarizes her experience with Signorelli's fresco this way: "To say this work of art had made a deep impression on me—as it had on Freud—would only be an understatement, for it changed the way I see the world."

Following are some meanings of the Antichrist: That as Jesus represented the Christ, so others can represent the opposite at different times in history. As Jesus taught love and forgiveness, others teach hate and revenge; as Jesus represented the good and the sacred, others stand for the bad and for evil; as Jesus represented joy and peace, others can bring darkness, strife and war; as Jesus represented justice and compassion, others can represent injustice and chaos, greed and envy. As Jesus represented dignity for the lowest in society and therefore democracy, others can represent narcissism and autocracy.

My being struck in my gut on seeing Signorelli's painting of the Antichrist and shouting out "Donald Trump" is not fully accurate.

It is not just Donald Trump, alas! It is the entire MAGA movement that puts hatred ahead of our better angels. Arrogance — including anthropocentrism and choosing to be oblivious of climate change and the destruction of Mother Earth as well as racism; sexism (which includes patriarchal values of dominance and power-over); violence; arousing of fear; advancing of avarice and greed that birth consumer capitalism and corporate capitalism both of which need to be consciously and deliberately held in check by laws that serve the common good; attacks on science and knowledge itself; envy. All stand out as the energy driving the Antichrist movement.

The energies just named are the exact seven capital sins that I lay out in my book on evil. They correspond to the shadow side of the seven chakras which I also name there.

Evil. Humanity's attraction to evil. That is what the archetype of the "Antichrist" names. Evil is not stupid; it is smart; and it goes to where the power lies. Such places as the Supreme Court; and the presidency; and Wall Street; and Media; and academia; and religion; and places in between. But it begins, alas!, in the human heart.

Evil has an agenda to spread. Lies are important to that agenda. Truth needs to be disregarded. By ignoring truth, one makes justice impossible—as Aquinas says, "the proper objects of the heart are truth and justice." Truth and justice travel together. The search for truth is necessary in our search for justice. To dismantle one is to dismantle the other. The forces of Antichrist know that.

Which is what Jesus tried to address. But he by no means stopped there. He took on a Roman empire and those pseudo-religious leaders in bed with the empire. Together, they crucified him for it. And many who have taken his teachings to heart have been similarly treated by the reigning powers of the day—just as he said would happen in his preaching of the Beatitudes. The Antichrist is not just the opposite of Christ and the values the Christ teaches—he/they want to displace the Christ and substitute themselves in its place.

The "Glorification of the Chosen" and the "Descent into Hades" are depicted on the wall opposite the Antichrist. It appears the Antichrist does not have the last word.

CHAPTER FIVE

JESUS AND DEMOCRACY

Does Jesus have something to say about democracy? Does the archetype of the "Christ" (or Buddha Nature or *Tselem* or image of God) have something to say about democracy? I think the answer is Yes.

I am not talking about faux religion or faux Christianity—in fact I am talking about the opposite of "Christian nationalism" and the notion that "we must put the commandments on classroom walls of public schools" and "we-must-teach-the-Bible-in-school" kind of Christianity. Or a Christianity that bows down to a person like Donald Trump as a leader. I may be old fashioned, but I don't think anyone who wants to put his political opponents in jail or talks about "grabbing women by their private parts" or has been convicted of sexual abuse by courts (and fined $84 million for his transgression) or found to be guilty by a jury of his peers of 34 felonies for writing checks to pay off a porn star to keep her silent during a presidential election or who makes it a practice to lie on an everyday basis is in any way a carrier of values that I want to represent me as a president. Or to be a role model for my children.

Nor would I want as president in 2024 a person who spoke to a group of donors from the fossil fuel corporations and promised them that if they were to give his campaign "one billion dollars" he would respond in kind and eliminate current laws that favor the curbing of fossil fuels to save the planet. In other words, "Mother Earth be damned!" The future of our children and grandchildren be damned so that one elderly person's short-term career and narcissism can be advanced.

And I certainly would not want such a person to pretend to represent Christ or say he is speaking in Christ's name. I do not think Jesus would countenance anyone who would sell his soul to the highest bidder in exchange for killing Mother Earth and all her children with increased fossil fuel enflaming of climate change—a reality of our time that is already causing untold misery for millions of people and species by setting heat records every year and threatening the stability and survival of our planet as we know it.

Does Jesus teach about democracy? And does Christ represent democracy in some way?

Thomas Aquinas (1225-1274) thought so: "Christ teaches the dignity of human nature… and the full participation in Divinity which is truly humanity's happiness and the goal of human life." Aquinas' brother Meister Eckhart (1260-1329) also thought so. He teaches about democracy and traces it to the teachings of Jesus about the dignity—indeed the "nobility" or "royalty" of ordinary people that was at the heart of Jesus' preaching. To preach about the immediate presence of the "kingdom" or reign of God is to preach about the nobility and royalty available to all. Eckhart recognizes that the teaching of Jesus on love and justice leads to equality and therefore democracy.

Eckhart is celebrating the theme of the "royal 'person" as found in the Scriptures. The royal person in Israel was responsible for justice and for keeping the community together. But we are all royal persons, Eckhart is insisting. We share in the dignity and nobility of royalty—but also in the responsibility for justice and compassion and keeping community together.

We all share in this dignity. By our divine origin as images of God and as creatures of the Creator, we ourselves are already nobles, aristocrats and of royal blood. "Our Lord teaches us in these words how royal people have been created in their nature." In us, "God's image shines and gives off light." No doubt he has the psalmist's hymn to creation in mind:

> "You have made them little less than God,
> and crowned them with glory and honor,
> you have given them dominion over the works of your hand,
> putting all things under their feet" (Ps 8:5f).

Thus the psalmist—and Eckhart—see all humans as kings. The Yahwist tradition "presents human beings as kings" throughout the Bible, points out biblical scholar Helen Kenik, who has written extensively on the theme of royal personhood in the Hebrew Bible. In the last analysis, only God is king, so this is another way of talking about our godliness and divinity. Here lies the bedrock to democracy: The dignity and divinity of each person from birth.

Eckhart invokes the metaphor of a "large eagle" that the prophet Ezechiel describes (Ez. 17:4f): "What our Lord calls a royal person is named by the prophet a large eagle. Who then is more royal than one who was born, on the one hand, from the highest and best that a creature possesses and, on the other hand, from the most intimate depths of the divine nature and its wilderness? Through the prophet Hosea our Lord says: 'I am going to lure her and lead her out into the wilderness and speak to her heart' (Ho 2:16). One with one, one from one, one in one, and eternally one in one. Amen." We are all born "from the highest and best that a creature possesses" and from "the most intimate depths of the divine nature and its wilderness." Here lie our origins, our noble and divine origins. We need to reflect on our noble origins to recover how the divine rests inside all of us.

Furthermore, in Eckhart's German, the words noble (*edler*) and eagle *(Alder)* are almost the same, so he is clearly playing with language in this commentary on the eagle and our origins being so noble. Eagles soar, there is no one above them. (This is especially so before the invention of the airplane. Eagles represented the beings that soared highest above the earth.) If no one is above one, then no one has the right to lord over us. That is democracy too.

If we are so noble, then an equality ought to reign between us all. We should all be treated as equals in our basic rights and needs and treat others as equals. That is a premise of democracy—"all men are created equal" said Thomas Jefferson in his opening line of the Declaration of Independence. Clearly, this was an aspiration and not a reality in his day since slaves were not considered equal nor were women even mentioned. It took great work and considerable time for these groups to claim their equality. But the goal, the aspiration, was planted early and like a seed it had to grow and blossom through a civil war and constitutional amendments and civil rights fights and through struggles for women's emancipation.

It follows, says Eckhart, that we need to "practice equality in human society." Here is how he puts it: "Since then Christ's whole nobility belongs equally to us all and is equally near to us, to him as much as to me...you must understand that, if someone wants to come by this gift equally to receive this good and the common nature which is equally near to all people, you must needs practice the same equality in human society, being no nearer to yourself than to another, just as in human nature there is nothing alien, nothing farther or nearer." Thus we recognize a societal relationship that develops from a personal relationship with one's self.

If we are brothers and sisters in one God, then we are all equals. This is the springboard for compassion. "You are to love, esteem, and consider all people like yourself, what happens to another, be it bad or good, should be for you as if it happened to you." All love demands equality. "Love will never be anything else than there where equality and unity are. Between a master and his servant there is no peace because there is no real equality." Peace and tranquility among peoples demand their equality.

For Eckhart, the same holds for personal relations and for marriage. "A wife and a husband are not alike, but in love they are equal." Where equality is lacking, we are to bring it forth. "There can be no love where love does not find equality or does not create equality." Societal leadership is of the same ilk. "If I were to lead people, they would never follow me with pleasure if they did not receive equality with me. For a movement or a deed is never accomplished with pleasure in the absence of equality."

Thus Eckhart, writing 450 years before Thomas Jefferson, has a far broader understanding of democracy than he did. For Eckhart does not limit the dignity of personhood to white people or to men or to men with property as did Jefferson in practice if not on paper. For Eckhart, we are born noble—all of us—and it is from that royalty, that our rights derive and we in turn are urged to treat others as ourselves and live "equally." This sense of equal dignity was of course ruptured by slavery and by patriarchy but in Eckhart's view, based on the teachings of Jesus, "there can be no love where love does not find equality or does not create equality."

Here lies both Eckhart's and Jesus' teachings about democracy. There has been, in human history, an unfolding or development of these basic principles. And the work of finding and making equality continues. Not to pursue it is to be unchristlike. It is to be Antichrist therefore.

Christ in glory by Beato Angelico (Orvieto Cathedral).

The preaching and deeds of the Antichrist by Luca Signorelli (Orvieto Cathedral).

The preaching and deeds of the Antichrist, detail.

The preaching and deeds of the Antichrist, detail.

The resurrection of the flesh by Luca Signorelli (Orvieto Cathedral).

The damned in hell by Luca Signorelli (Orvieto Cathedral).

The blessed in heaven by Luca Signorelli (Orvieto Cathedral).

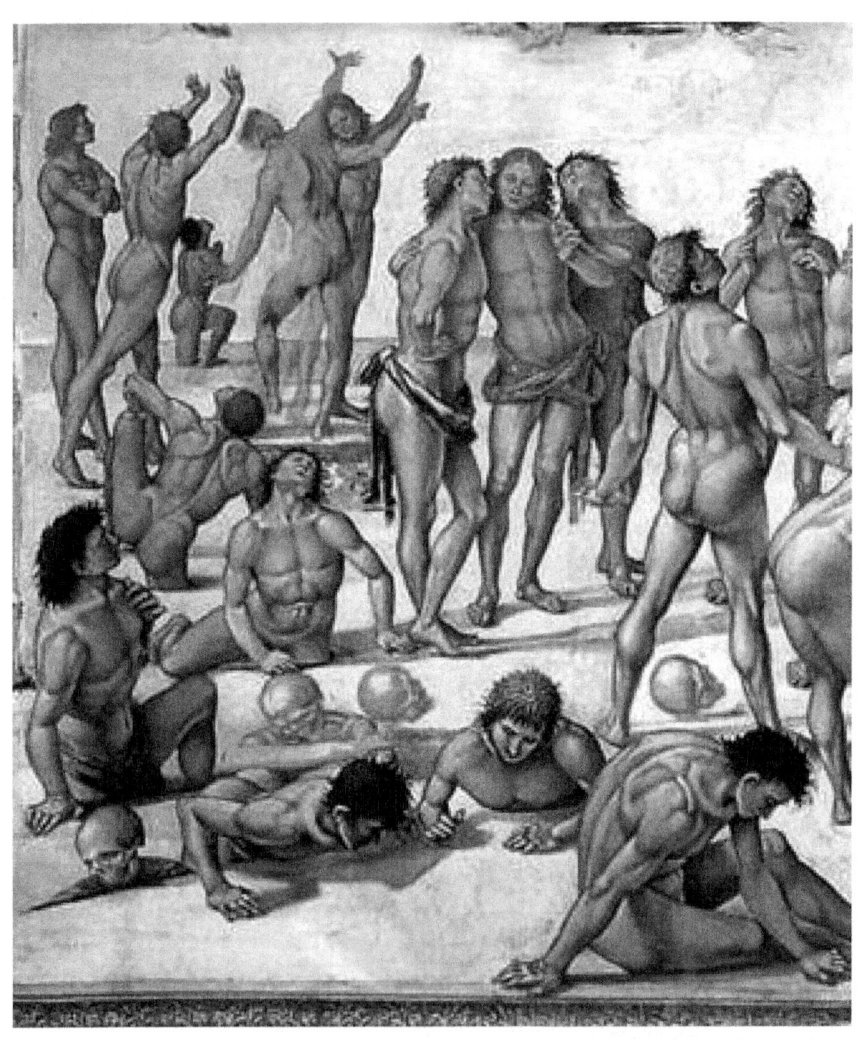

The resurrection of the flesh, detail.

The blue man by Hildegard of Bingen.

The Antichrist by Hildegard of Bingen.

CHAPTER SIX

MAGA: MAKING AMERICA GROTESQUE AGAIN

Some want to believe that MAGA stands for Making America Great Again. But I propose that what it really means is Making America Grotesque Again.

Grotesque like when American slave ships—probably over 36,000 in number—made voyages across the sea filled with human cargo for the slave trade. This "Middle Passage" transported about 12.5 million slaves of which 1.8 million died en route. The others landed in a new land with a new language to serve an old purpose: be slaves and unpaid workers for life. And be treated as less than human with families broken up at will. And one's children and descendants treated the same, so that this new country might have a strong—and cheap—labor force. And so it was.

Grotesque like the Civil War that was fought for four years over whether slavery would persist or not. Over 750,000 Americans, both north and south, were killed or maimed in that war. But the North won and kept its army in the South to guarantee that freed blacks would have their freedom. The 12th, 13th and 14th amendments to the constitution were passed to guarantee those rights for ex-slaves.

But a grotesque compromise was effected by President Rutherford Hayes in 1877 who, to get elected, promised to recall the Union Troops. And an era of grotesque Jim Crow Laws and lynchings and intimidation and denial of voting rights and other rights was enacted. White supremacy ruled and endured for all practical purposes through two world wars and the Korean War (all of which black citizens fought and died in) right up to the Supreme Court's decision in 1952 that segregation of schools was unconstitutional. The Civil Rights movement followed (1956-1966) because that law was resisted so fiercely.

Grotesque insofar as those civil rights laws, which included the right to vote freely, were gradually dismantled by Chief Justice John Roberts and the Supreme Court beginning in 2013 right up through today.

Grotesque insofar as genocide toward the first peoples on this land was carried out throughout American history. Wars were fought, multiple treaties were broken, lies compounded, reservations created and forced marches enacted to remove tribes from their own historical roots and sacred lands to places that were less bountiful. In no way were native peoples treated with the dignity and equality they deserved as human beings.

Grotesque insofar as tribes were often moved again when oil or some other valuable resource was discovered on their reservations.

Grotesque insofar as in the largest state in the union, indigenous peoples in the 19th century, by fiat from the governor of California, were not only driven off their lands but were hunted with a bounty on their heads of $50 per Indian killed. Governmental and church schools were set up beginning in Pennsylvania and children snatched from their parents and tribe were sent to these schools where there was considerable physical, mental, and even sexual abuse.

Grotesque insofar as 30 million buffalo once roamed the plains of America, but that number was reduced to 500 (sic) in the 19th century in the insane and pathological attempt to wipe out Native Americans by wiping out their nearest four-legged companions.

Grotesque insofar as trauma haunts both the indigenous and black communities to this day because of these past actions to individuals and communities and families.

Grotesque insofar as Chinese peoples, many of whom were brought over in the 19th century to help construct the railroads, were forbidden to bring women or spouses with them and then (with unions being complicit) were forbidden to get work in industry and to vote or become citizens. The Page Act of 1875 forbade any Chinese women from entering the country. The Exclusion Laws forbidding them citizenship were in effect up to 1943.

Grotesque because for Asians too, there was the experience and threat of lynchings such as occurred in Los Angeles in 1871 where 18 men were lynched and riots in Seattle in 1886 resulted in hundreds of Chinese being forcibly put on ships and returned to China.

Grotesque for Japanese citizens who were rounded up in 1942, forced to abandon their homes and places of business and work and sent to concentration camps for the duration of the war. Only in 1988 did the US government formally apologize.

Grotesque therefore for its recurrent racism including redlining and other strategies employed to prevent people of color from owning their own homes, the number one source of stable income for most Americans.

Grotesque because states such as Florida are passing laws currently that forbid the teaching of these facts we have considered in this list of grotesque atrocities, and they are being cheered on by the MAGA movement –Make America Grotesque Again— otherwise known as the Republican Party.

Grotesque insofar as the economic discrepancies between the haves and have-nots are expanding in our time. Tax breaks for billionaires and corporations under President Trump resulted in adding $7.8 trillion to the national debt. This debt is being paid on the back of middle Americans. Billionaires on the average pay only 8% tax on their earnings—and many, thanks to their influence in passing legislation through dark money or by donating to candidates and political parties and their army of lawyers—pay zero taxes. Meanwhile, the average citizen pays 14.9% in taxes per year. Yet the billionaires avail themselves of all the public works— schools, roads, bridges, airports, railroad, government workers, courts, police, etc.—that ordinary citizens do, the same ordinary citizens who pick up the vast majority of the costs.

Grotesque because of the immense power billionaires have at their disposal to influence legislation and courts and media. They are overrepresented on the courts of the land and especially the Supreme Court where a number have been clearly bought by way of lavish gifts and other enticements. Yet citizens have no way to appeal gross corruption since the Court accepts no limits on its transgressions and tells the country to take it by faith that they are busy policing themselves.

SCOTUS of late has taken a wrecking ball to democracy and the American Constitution and to Jesus' notion of the dignity of all peoples. Under the leadership of Chief Justice John Roberts, SCOTUS has become an integral member of the MAGA cult. It is rendering America grotesque again by allowing dark money to flood American politics so billionaires and large corporations effectively dictate what issues are before the court and how many decisions are decided. In its recent Chevron decision, it seeks to emasculate the EPA to the delight of fossil fuel barons (not future generations of creatures wanting to survive on an ever-hotter planet). It has effectively gutted the voting rights act that Dr. King and others died for 60 years ago. It has robbed women of decision-making over their own bodies and unleashed horror stories of 12-year-old rape victims forced to flee their state and women with complications during their pregnancies being unable to find medical help. This same court, so eager to throw overboard laws that have been precedent for decades, has done nothing to interfere with corruption of two of its judges who accepted millions of dollars of gifts from billionaire sugar daddies with decisions before the court.

All this qualifies distinctly as grotesque—a grotesque scenario of so-called justice and the grotesque picture of justices who appear accountable to no one. No wonder they eagerly approved of a plan whereby an American president cannot be subject to the law for any "official acts" undertaken while in office and even when he/she leaves office. This is how they envision their own role, so the president should not be subject to the law anymore than they are. The respect for the court and therefore the rule of law is in free fall and for good reason. This is the most grotesque court since that of the time of the Dred Scott decision. That decision had everything to do with the Civil War that came three years later. Today's unsupreme court, so wrapped in its ideologies masquerading as jurisprudence, is an active agent in the democracide in vogue among the fascism of today. "Institutional violence" (Susan Sontag's definition of fascism) is alive and well at SCOTUS. And, of course, christofascism. All this qualifies as Antichrist.

All this grotesqueness is Antichrist at work. It is the opposite of the values that Jesus taught, and Christ-followers ought to practice. There is a grotesque distortion of religion and of Christianity going on when slavery, racism, injustice, favoritism, monied power reign. It is not an effort at a kingdom of God, but a caricature of such a promised kingdom. It is a kingdom of the Antichrist on earth, therefore.

CHAPTER SEVEN

18 SIGNS OF THE TIMES: THE ANTICHRIST IN AMERICAN POLITICS, 2024

To "read the signs of the times" is one of the requirements of being a spiritual person. Jesus admonishes us to do so in the Gospel and French theologian M. D. Chenu considers it part and parcel of how the Spirit works in us all. The phrase was readily employed at the Second Vatican Council which was called by Pope John XXIII to "open the window" to a fuller dialog between religion and the modern world. Here we will name eighteen "signs of the times" that name how the Antichrist is at work currently in our culture in the presidential year 2024.

Such a reflection as this is not unheard of in the tradition of employing the Antichrist archetype. Luca Signorelli's fresco in Orvieto is not shy about including persons of his time. Even Christopher Columbus has a prominent place in that painting. This seems to be ample invitation for us, living in the final months before a presidential election in America in 2024, to name the Antichrist scene of our day. In this chapter I intend to do so not so much by naming names (though there may be a few that arise) as by naming issues and causes that seem to contradict the teachings of Christ and the teachings of democracy in a blatant manner. The Antichrist does not have to be a particular person—it can also be a movement, a gathering of persons, who may have sold their soul for a prize of hanging out with a modern-day Antichrist. In the process, one's ego or eagerness for revenge or lust for power benefits mightily. What we know from Signorelli's painting and from Hildegard's treatment of the Antichrist is that the Antichrist is alluring to the extreme and is enticing and can attract millions to act against their own self-interests and their better natures.

After all, this is 2024, the season of i-phones and social media and Tik Tok and Instagram. Via multiple gadgets we can listen to Antichrist messaging happening in countless forums from all over the world. And the situation is not just about who is listening but also about who is speaking. In our time the Antichrist speaker is not on a platform as in the 16th century painting we are considering, but can choose multiple modes of getting his message out. His message? Signorelli tells us in his painting that it is the devil's message; he who has the ear of the Antichrist is preaching in tandem with the Antichrist.

We offer a list of signs of the Antichrist in our time. Of course, this is a partial and not an exhaustive list for the examples can be as varied as is human imagination for malfeasance. Among the messages being announced by today's Antichrist we find the following 18:

1. A countless stream of lies. At the June debate with President Biden, ex-president Donald Trump was clocked afterwards by neutral observers as having told 27 lies in about 45 minutes of talking (since Biden spoke about 45 minutes also in the 90-minute debate). This should come as no surprise since the *Washington Post* counted at least 33,000 lies that Trump offered the American people during his four-year presidency. One of the first—and I remember how shocked the press was at the time—was at the very beginning when he took the oath of office and told his press secretary to say the next day that it was the biggest crowd at any presidential inauguration in history. This was simply not true, and photos showed his audience compared for example to the audience on the occasion of President Obama's initial inauguration. There was no comparison.

Is lying important? Yes it is. There is a reason why Satan is called the "father of lies." If we cannot rely on mutual truth-telling, there can be no authentic discourse or sharing after all. As we have seen, Aquinas teaches that "the proper objects of the heart are truth and justice." Truth and justice ride together. Lies and injustice also travel as companions. Lies pave the way to injustice. Lies are not a path to justice and justice is what keeps societies together. Truth—or the reach for it—are glue to relationships of all kinds. When someone lies, one is playing footloose with reality. Lying can be a form of control and domination—dominating even truth and truthful discourse. It breaks down the very art of communication. The Antichrist is characterized by lying.

2. Project 2025. An example of a significant lie from the Antichrist corner is this: on July 5, 2024, Donald Trump posted on social media that he knows nothing about Project 2025, the fascist document laying out what a Trump administration will do if elected to office. "That's an obvious lie," remarks Civic Shout begging people to sign a petition "urging media outlets to stop parroting Trump's lies." The article points out how some of Trump's top advisors such as Stephen Miller and Johnny McEntee are "top architects of the Project 2025 agenda." Trump's SuperPAC is actually running ads promoting Project 2025 and calling it "Trump's Project 2025." Many political reporters it seems are "taking Trump's lie at face value and helping spread the lie that Trump has nothing to do with Project 2025." Again, lies are integral to the Antichrist.

3. Stormy Daniels trial. A lie Trump has spoken on many occasions, and which played prominently in his recent conviction of 34 counts of felony in the hush payment trial for Stormy Daniels was that he never had sex with her. But she testified under oath and in considerable detail about what their encounter was like and offered multiple details of the room where it took place. Twelve jurors concluded that she was telling the truth and Trump, who chose not to testify under oath, was not telling the truth. The Antichrist refuses to tell the truth.

4. The 2020 elections. The biggest and most consequential lie in Trump's repertoire is surely the lie that the 2020 election was rigged, and that Biden lost. He took that lie to 63 individual courts around the country and not one agreed with him. Moreover, there is explicit testimony that he knew he lost the election but nevertheless kept peddling this Big Lie the consequences of which are immense because, as mentioned above, no society can survive on lies as a foundation. It is this "Big Lie" that fired up the thousands of people who invaded the Capitol on January 6 to interfere with the peaceful transfer of power to a new and duly elected presidential team. This lie resulted therefore in the death of seven people and the injury of 114 officers alone who were defending the Capitol and the congress people inside. In addition, over 1000 people are now in prison because they followed Trump's lies and invaded the capitol building. Since Christ is called "Truth," lies are integral to an Antichrist movement.

5. Eliminating protections. Another dimension pertaining to the Antichrist is that of taking power from those who are experts in fields that affect the general public and putting power into the hands of people who are not. In a thoughtful article entitled "Six Corporate-Owned US Supreme Court Justices Have Completed Their Assigned Mission," former labor secretary Robert Reich points out that conservatives love to denounce the "administrative state" and its regulations. But what is really meant by "administrative state" is "agencies tasked with protecting the public from corporations that seek profits at the expense of the health, safety, and pocketbooks of average Americans."

The word "protection" is more to the point than "regulation" therefore. We are dealing with the moral and spiritual issue of greed — corporate greed where the "bottom line" is all-important, a kind of idol or golden calf in itself that can mow over the rights and lives of everyday citizens. "Regulations are the means by which agencies translate broad legal mandates into practical guardrails."

People need clean air and clean water, but the "corporate legal movement" readily mobilizes to accomplish their ends at the expense of the basic needs of ordinary citizens.

SCOTUS recently made a decision in the Chevron case that rendered it far more difficult for regulators to regulate and assured a "far more costly and laborious process" of suing corporations in federal courts before juries. "Countless" — and expensive corporate lawsuits will follow because of this decision that overturned a 40-year old precedent. "Make no mistake: Consumers, workers, and ordinary Americans will be hurt by these decisions. Big corporations — especially their top executives and major investors — will make even more money than they're already making because of them."

This decision was born of a corporate strategy launched 53 years ago when corporations complained of being "under attack" from consumer, labor, and environmental groups. A "tidal wave" of corporate money rushed into American politics creating a corporate legal movement of lobbyists, lawyers, political operatives, public relations, media gurus and think tanks like the American Enterprise Institute, the Heritage Foundation and the Federalist Society. Among the young lawyers working for the conservative legal movement at that time were today's Chief Justice John Roberts, and justices Clarence Thomas and Samuel Alito. Trump's three recent appointments to SCOTUS were also from that same corporate legal movement and were nominated to the Court by Leonard Leo, a billionaire operative with the Federalist Society.

Reich concludes: "Corporate capitalism in the United States has always coexisted uneasily with democratic capitalism." He asks: Which is in charge—big corporations or the people? It seems big corporations are winning.

This is an Antichrist trend insofar as it is averse to equality and fairness and government of, by, and for the people. Instead, it serves the corporations, their investors, and their well-paid lackeys.

6. Denial of climate change and refusal to work to combat it. This is integral to the work of the Antichrist. I do not think one need argue the case that a healthy earth is inherent to a belief in a God of creation who loves that creation. If "God is love," this love extends to all creatures and all persons—and especially the poor and vulnerable and dispossessed. All persons and creatures need healthy food and soil, waters, air, forests. And protection from exploitation and excessive heating of the planet that comes with climate change. As we saw above, that protection can readily be sold to the highest bidder.

Heat waves are setting records in America and around the world. Seas are rising, hurricanes are becoming more severe, wildfires are multiplying and droughts as well as floods are on the rise. The MAGA movement has next to nothing to say about climate change and its solutions other than to forbid, as they have in Florida and more and more states, government employees to mention the term "climate change" in any of their *official documents.* Consider that in the campaign of 2024, Donald Trump told a group of fossil fuel CEOs behind closed doors that if they would give his campaign one billion dollars he would see to it that environmental laws passed in the previous administration were gutted. There is nothing subtle about this pledge. The MAGA slogan is, "Drill, baby, drill!"

Denying and ignoring climate change is the greatest insult to God the Creator. It endangers all life on the planet —so much for being "pro-life." And it is matricide—the ultimate act of hatred to our Mother, Mother Earth. It is deeply misogynistic and ecocidal as well, the killing of our common home.

One of the promises of "Project 2025," the blueprint for a Trump presidency put out by the Heritage Foundation we saw in section two above is to eliminate programs, disembowel bureaus, and end reporting on anything climate related.

Who, what, is the Heritage Foundation? In an article entitled, "Meet the group behind Trump's fascist 2025 agenda," *Daily Kos* staff member Mark Sumner informs us of how Heritage Foundation began in 1973 by the founder of Coors Brewing and conservative strategists Paul Weyrich and Ed Feulner. They felt that President

Richard Nixon had "moved too far to the left" and other Republican organizations were also "too timid." Today's version of the Heritage Foundation is "thrilled by the Supreme Court's recent immunity ruling" and committed to attacking diversity and equity initiatives. They are also linked up with the religious fascist Opus Dei movement. As one recent study notes, Roberts, architect of Project 2025 and president of Heritage Foundation "has close ties" with the Opus Dei center in Washington DC, "a hub of activity for the radical and secretive Catholic group." Issues like forbidding birth control and disdaining separation of church and state are high on their agenda. A long-time goal of "penetrating Washington's political and legal elite" has come to success "through its close association with men like Kevin Roberts and Leonard Leo."

President Roberts promises not to kill all leftists—"as long as we sit quietly and acquiesce to their dominion over the nation." How kind of them to allow us to have our lives "in exchange for our freedom"! Today's Heritage Foundation "is a much more dangerous beast" than that of old. "It has wealth. It has connections. And it has democracy in its sights."

This too is gist for an Antichrist movement. The Antichrist cheers on contributions to ecocide and matricide, the killing of the ecosystems that support all of life and the killing of Mother Earth as we know her.

7. Dark money taking over. Dark money is a tool of Antichrist for sure. Senator Sheldon Whitehouse puts it this way: "It's a trifecta: dark money is behind climate denial, Court capture and corruption of Congress—one crew, one plan, one cancer in the body politic." He recognizes that this all came to pass with the passing of the *Citizens United* decision by the Supreme Court. Dark money has provided a "filthy bestiary of influence" since that time. Dark money is the "massive anonymous political spending by special interests" who hide their identities from the public. Voters become less important in deciding political outcomes and "the big secret spenders" become more important. Front groups such as "donors trusts" and 501c3s and c4s and superPACs dominate. Yet polling is "off the charts" to restrict this kind of dark money—republicans as well as independents and democrats are against it.

Whitehouse points out that before *Citizens United*, climate change was a bipartisan issue (in 2008 McCain included it in his platform), but fossil-fuel dark money killed that bipartisanship. The "amenable" justices on the Supreme Court–including for sure chief justice John Roberts—were captured by a dark-money operation funded by "creepy polluter billionaires and managed by their creepy minion Leonard Leo." Thanks to the Heritage Foundation, the Supreme Court members are instructed on what to do to keep dark money flowing.

Dark money is an important tool in the campaign of the Antichrist.

8. Racism and "Christian" nationalism. The Antichrist is and always has been committed to institutionalizing racism. One recent example is a Mississippi lawmaker who seeks to eliminate all state funding to Historically Black Colleges and Universities in his state. State senator John Polk has introduced legislation with narrow restrictions that would apply to just three schools in the state— each of them just happens to be a black college or university.

The very term "Christian nationalism" is a contradiction in terms if one understands Jesus' teachings at all. Jesus said "preach good news to all nations" and did not endorse one community alone.

Of course, behind the term "Christian nationalism" is another adjective—"white." Racism is baked into that term and its practice, and all the Antichrist stands for. Racism divides since clearly the human species is diverse in color of skin and varied ethnicities. All racism denies the diversity of creation, evolution's diversity and the Creator's intentions. It is a capital sin in opposition to the first chakra (which, being about vibration, applies to our relationships to the universe and all creation since all atoms in the universe are vibrating). Racism is a cover and a tool for one group to lord over other groups. It is born of fear and of a superiority complex dangerous for its tribalism and blind to the gifts that diversity brings. The dangerous notion of a "master race" is born of such sentiments and deserves to be confronted wherever it raises its very ugly head. It has been said that MAGA legislators "up and down the ballot are racing to repeal the last century of progress toward equality."

The 2025 Project embraces Trump's notion of white male privilege and Christian nationalism and will be expressed in a "whole of government" offensive against the "Great Awakening" and supposed "totalitarian cult" that has subverted American institutions. "All traces of DEI (diversity, equity, and inclusion) programs will be eradicated." Antichrist commits to racism.

9. **Christofascism.** Christian nationalism culminates in Christofascism. Christofascism preaches violence in the name of a so-called "Christ." Christofascism takes the essence of fascism and wraps it in Christ-language. For example, Susan Sontag defines fascism as "institutional violence." It follows that Christofascism would be institutional violence in the name of Christ. The essence of fascism is control and power-over. Sadism therefore is intrinsic

people, who were literally running for their lives, reported afterwards that they thought they were going to be killed.

Seven people died from that riot and hundreds were injured and so far over 1000 have gone to prison. It was violent—just as the Antichrist likes it. And anti-democratic—just as the Antichrist likes. And, since the whole purpose was to interfere with a valid election, it was profoundly anti-democratic. Just as the Antichrist approves of.

Donald Trump, who has repeatedly called for Hillary Clinton to be jailed and suggested that retired General Mark Milley should be executed, seems quite at home with violence. The Antichrist uses violence and threatens violence readily.

12. So-called Abortion laws. A compulsion to control women's bodies seems to constitute a large part of fascism and Christofascism. Thus, a preoccupation with abortion and contraception rules the mindsets of many MAGA adherents. There was nothing in the Roe v. Wade bill of the land that held sway for 49 years and that Trump's Supreme Court overthrew (citing two witch-burning lawyers from England in the 17th century in doing so) that insisted that a woman have an abortion. Nothing at all. A woman who is against abortion is not bound to have one. But there are times when a woman needs an abortion—for example if her pregnancy is going awry—and now, post-Roe, many states have passed very harsh abortion bands. We are hearing horrendous stories of women suffering and coming close to death or being forced to flee their state to get the medical treatment they require. The same is true of victims of rape—including as we have seen—a 12-year-old Ohio girl who was raped and had to leave her state to get an abortion. The fallout and collateral damage for women and girls from the Supreme Court decision to gut Roe v Wade is very frightening indeed. Some states such as Florida have passed laws forbidding abortion after six weeks, and this is especially disturbing since many women do not even know if they are pregnant at six weeks.

Why all this compulsion to control women's bodies? Why all this righteousness and sureness that male politicians—and not doctors—are knighted to tell women what they can and cannot do with their bodies?

To me, the abortion question has been hijacked by patriarchy itself: a view that men know what is best for women including their most intimate decisions regarding their own bodies is disturbing. Isn't it time to finally leave such thinking in the past? I do not see this to be in any way Christlike. It is the opposite. It is the way of the Antichrist therefore.

13. Sexual obsessions. A preoccupation with sex, which invariably makes itself known wherever patriarchy is dominant, is, it seems to me, a sign of sickness and of being stuck in adolescence. It is a refusal to grow up. Pope Francis criticized those who "put all their theology in a condom" which is quite vivid language for what I am talking about. It seems to me that Antichrist would be delighted to freeze adult minds in an adolescent world view—this way adult issues of justice, injustice, service to the common good would take second place to sexual hallucinations.

Adult moral issues include concerns about not just the body but the body politic as well. About justice, therefore. And about love-justice which is the biblical meaning for love. As Jose Miranda has put it, speaking from the context of Latin America where the struggle for justice is so pronounced, "one of the most disastrous errors in the history of Christianity is to have tried—under the influence of Greek definitions—to differentiate between love and justice." The Biblical tradition brings both together. Meister Eckhart echoes this when he declares that "compassion is where peace and justice kiss." And "compassion means justice." The prophets were passionate about justice and injustice. They saw the latter as the undoing of the balance of creation which stands on two pillars: justice and righteousness, the latter being internalized justice. Separating love from justice is part of the Antichrist agenda, and appealing to sexual obsessions creates an enticing distraction for that very purpose.

14. A blueprint for destruction of democracy. The goal of MAGA is, in the words of Heritage president Kevin D. Roberts, to be about "Institutionalizing Trumpism." That is exactly what Project 2025 is about: To lay out a blueprint for President Trump if he is re-elected in November 2024. Roberts also declared that blood will not be spilled so long as those who disagree sit by and lets things come to pass as Project 2025 dictates. (See number 11 above.) Project 2025 represents a concerted effort to gather Trump's revenge and resentments into policy. Project 2025 is an about 900-page handbook that spells out how this will come to be in a MAGA administration. They call it *Mandate for Leadership*. Where will it lead? How will we get there?

Some of the highlights include the following: rounding up and deporting millions of immigrants, pardoning the January 6 offenders, prosecuting Trump's prosecutors, imposing tariffs on all imports including 60 percent on goods from China, and "Drill, baby, drill!" The latter referring of course to supporting fossil fuel companies long and hard, the future of Mother Earth be damned. Robert L. Borosage, writing about "Why Trump's Second Victory

Would Be Worse," in *The Nation* on June 4, 2024, tells us that the policy proposal of Project 2025 will prove to be "more assault than agenda" and labels it a "chilling guidebook" to a second Trump term.

An immediate executive order—Schedule F from the last weeks of Trump's previous presidency "will be revived, empowering the president to turn the civil service into a spoils system." Instead of the usual 4,000 workers, his new administration will create 20,000 to 50,000 political appointees beholden to Trump alone. Loyalty, not expertise or experience, will be the hallmark of these hires. Key to it all will be "squelching any independence in the Department of Justice" and of course filling the courts with reactionary partisans—something we have learned the hard way they are very adept at. It is one of the charisms of the Heritage Foundation.

Using the National Guard and building detention camps to hold them all, millions of undocumented workers will be rounded up for deportation. To hell with the many jobs they do in the American economy that other Americans do not want to do. Will this not crash the economy as well as destroy families altogether?

"All traces of DEI (diversity, equity, and inclusion) programs will be eradicated" along with all mention of gender. No abortion and no birth control will be tolerated other than abstinence. Will gay marriage be eliminated also?

All action on climate change will cease. Plans to eliminate programs and disembowel bureaus and end reporting on anti-climate actions are spelled out in detail.

There will be more tax cuts for corporations and the very rich and more deregulation of agencies that protect our water, air, food, workplaces, drugs, manufacturing and pocketbooks. This has already received a big boost from the recent supreme court Chevron decision. "Trump's government will throw a truly bacchanalian orgy for entrenched interests: Big Oil, Big Pharma, Big Ag, the military-industrial complex, Wall Street, and more."

To achieve all this will require undermining American elections on which democracy depends. Elections will be arranged to always "come out the right way" since, as we well know by now, Trump does not believe in losing elections. Gerrymandering will flourish even more, voting rights be curtailed further, and dark money flow ever faster and furiouser. Voting rights that the civil rights movement marched and protested and went to jail for and died for sixty years ago will be erased.

Democracide, the killing of democracy, is going on by Trump and MAGA followers and by Chief Justice Roberts and SCOTUS. Decisions to allow dark money to swamp elections and to gut the Voting Rights act and to destroy the EPA, FDA, and other agencies that protect our environment and health and have courts do it instead. All the enablers of Trump and MAGA who have sold their souls for power and participated in democracide—all that is Antichrist at work.

Of course, this whole project is wrapped in a pseudo-religious and pseudo-Christian panache—and this for a man who never finds himself in a church. Christofasism has no sense of shame. As one commentator put it, in his conclusion to an article on "The Theocratic Blueprint for Trump's Next Term," the "MAGA imperial presidency… is equal parts Cotton Mather and Roy Cohn."

If this is not the Antichrist at work, I don't know what is.

15. A fascist's paradise. The National Campaign for Justice offers further reflections on Project 2025. Among their observations are the following. They call the document "a 920-page roadmap to dictatorship" that outlines "exactly what Trump and his allies want out of a Trump second term. "To call it frightening is an understatement. It is not hyperbole to say it's a plan to end American democracy. It wants to destroy the separation of church and state and eliminate checks and balances in order to install an authoritative government run by an all powerful 'president.'" Of course, it recently received a green light and a blank check in hand thanks to the recent "unsupreme court" and its six unjustices' decision about an imperial and unchecked president who is immune from following laws—a king therefore.

Among its highlights are a nationwide abortion plan; jailing of political enemies; destroying the Department of education as well as the FDA, EPA, DFFB, NLRG and even the FBI. This would kill literally millions of people and the planet itself as we know it, at the same time that it ends American democracy. Truly the work of an Antichrist by any other name.

Among the more than 100 right-wing groups supporting and cheering on Project 2025 are fanatical extremists such as Moms for Liberty, and Tea Party Patriots, and dozens of additional anti-abortion and anti-LGBTQ+ groups including Family Research Council, American Family Association, the Heritage foundation, the American Legislative Exchange Council (ALEC), Turning Point USA and FreedomWorks. The national Campaign for Justice sums it up this way: "It's a christofascist's wish list of religion mixed with hate and bigotry" that is determined to take away fundamental rights of millions.

The New Republic states that Project 2025 is "a remarkably detailed guide to turning the United States into a fascist's paradise." Fascism and Christ are incompatible, therefore fascism is the work of the Antichrist.

16. Normalizing Hate. *The New Republic* states that "Trump's Reelection Agenda was set by actual hate groups." Three of the dozens of think tanks and advocacy groups who drew it up are hate groups officially designated as such by the Southern Poverty Law Center. Trump has recently tried to distance himself from the document but "these group's fingerprints were all over his last administration and will likely be all over his next one."

The first of these hate groups is the Alliance Defending Freedom, the conservative Christian legal advocacy group that brought the case that overturned Roe v. Wade. They also seek to recriminalize sexual actions between LGBTQ+ consenting adults and they are committed to spreading ugly disinformation about gay and trans people. Not incidentally, House Speaker Mike Johnson worked at their law firm for almost ten years. Former Trump attorney John Eastman also worked with the group and Trump invited the group's senior counsel Tyson Langhofer to speak at a youth outreach event in the White House in 2018.

A second designated hate group is the Center for Immigration Studies or CIS, a conservative antiimmigration think tank. Former White House advisor Stephen Miller, infamous for locking children up in cages, relied on them for much of the misinformation that he put on President Trump's desk. Fearmongering about immigrants is their trademark.

The third designated hate group is the Family Research Council famous for publishing anti-LGBTQ+ studies based on "debunked science" and opposing same-sex marriage. They have also slammed laws against hate crimes and anti-bullying programs. Trump has spoken to this group on several occasions.

It seems that Hate Groups and their handlers make fine candidates for Antichrist movements. Why wouldn't they? Hatred comes from the heart and is the obverse of love. Jesus and the Christ teach love— "Love your neighbor as yourself" and "God is love." Hatred in these groups is directed indiscriminately against any one or any group at all and not for reasons of justice but "merely because their disposition or character is not to our liking" and the punishment hatred seeks to meet out is without limits. "Hatred intends evil in itself to one's neighbor," as Thomas Aquinas instructs us. A sure sign of the Antichrist.

17. Support of Putin and other dictators. What does one say about supporting a dictator who tortures and kills his own political opponents, which Putin has done with Novotny and many others? And who squelches free press and murders journalists who do not adulate him? Or invades a sovereign country such as Ukraine and delivers untold suffering on the peoples there, killing tens of thousands, maiming hundreds of thousands, destroying entire cities in the process? And who threatens nuclear war and the rest of Europe? And who lives a lifestyle fit for a czar and instead of democracy depends on rich oligarchs to run a country rabid with corruption? And who, to win his war that defies all the norms of the United Nations established since WWII, saddles up to the North Korea dictator who abuses his own citizens and defies all imperatives from the United Nations and threatens nuclear war against his neighbors?

Donald Trump admires Putin and emulates him while bragging about how he and the North Korean dictator exchanged "love letters." He has also threatened to withdraw from NATO—which would clearly be the culmination of Putin's wet dream since NATO was set up 75 years ago to resist the Soviet Union from invading other countries after the war. Recently, while President Biden was addressing leaders from NATO countries, Trump was entertaining Hungarian president Viktor Orban, a Putin friend who has turned his country into a one-party republic. He is beloved by MAGA followers. Trump has promised to abandon the people of Ukraine and give Putin what he wants, and has invited Putin to "do whatever you want" to European neighbors.

Putin is just one of the many shady characters that Trump is at home with including many who live in the United States (a number of whom are now serving jail sentences or, like him, awaiting trial). Nor should we forget that Trump is a convicted felon 34 times over as well as a convicted sexual offender (to the tune of a $84 million sentence). Aquinas observes that "tyrants are more afraid of good people than of evil people." The Antichrist prefers bad people to good people.

18. Blasphemy/Idolatry. Many of the MAGA followers of Trump revere him as a religious figure, a head of their cult, and are engaged in nothing less than blasphemy and idol worship in the process. Following are a few headlines reminding us of that fact. "The Deification of Donald Trump Poses Some Interesting Questions" (*New York Times*). "Theologian Russell Moore Has a Message for Christians who Still Worship Donald Trump" (*Time Magazine*). "God, Guns & Trump: Jesus is their savior, Trump is their candidate" (*Montreal Gazzette*).

Journalist McKay Coppins has read every prayer offered at Trump's campaign events as he runs for president this cycle—58 in all. Some are "benign," others" blasphemous." All told, his Christian followers "now seem convinced that" Trump is anointed by God "to defeat the forces of evil and redeem the country."

Eight of ten Evangelicals voted for Trump in 2020 and that

percentage seems to be holding for 2024. They say he "shares their faith and values" even though Robert P. Jones, founder of PPRI or the Public Religion Research Institute, calls Trump's religious persona "outright fraud" and says he is "not only one of the least religious but also likely one of the most theologically ignorant presidents the country has ever had." It is said that he "infuses his campaign with Christian trappings." One Trumper supporting him, Kimberly Vaughn of Florence, Kentucky, joining a Trump rally near Dayton, Ohio, said, "Trump supports Jesus, and without Jesus, America will fall." At the rally many T-shirts and hats worn and sold proclaimed religious slogans like, "Jesus is my savior, Trump is my president" and "God, Guns & Trump" and "Make America Godly Again" with an image of a Jesus bathed in light resting his hands on Trump's shoulders. Nobody questions his hush payments to a porn star or his 34 felony convictions.

Recently, Trump sold an item called God Bless the USA Bible for $60 each and promoted it with a video wherein he proclaims, "We must make America pray again." In it one finds the King James Bible in largeprint "and—arguably sacrilegiously—the U.S. Constitution and the lyrics" to Republican cheerleader Lee Greenwood's GOP anthem, "God Bless the USA." Trump reported making $300,000 from hawking this item in a 2024 tax release.

What is that all about? One dimension is that the fundamentalist theology worships a punitive Father-God. Patriarchy is baked into the brand and Trump is nothing if not patriarchy unchained — patriarchal, angry, out for revenge, reptilian-brain-like and punitive.

Jim Guth, a political scientist at Furman University is an expert on the role of religion in politics. He has found that white evangelicals are "invariably the most populist" among people of faith and they have a "transactional relationship" with Trump. They exhibit a "pronounced form" of "strong Islamophobia, Christian nationalism, extreme moral traditionalism, opposition to trade pacts, militaristic attitudes, resistance to political compromise and climate change denial."

There are photos of evangelicals laying hands on Trump in the Oval Office which is a ritual done to ordain pastors or commission missionaries. Trump's convictions in court are interpreted as "signs of persecution" like Jesus underwent. Trump fans that fire by claiming, "they're not persecuting me. They're persecuting you." We are told that evangelicals "think that politics is a form of spiritual warfare and believe that God is using Donald Trump to help wage this war." A video called "God Made Trump" was posted on Truth Social and has run frequently at Trump campaign rallies and narrates how "God gave us Trump." A leader behind it characterizes himself as Christian and a man of faith but says he has never read the Bible and does not attend church. Eric Trump has exclaimed that his father "literally saved Christianity."

All this seems to be what is meant by both blasphemy and idolatry. Both are integral to the Antichrist at work.

A certain number is usually associated with the Antichrist: 666. Add up each digit in that number and the total is 18. That might have something to do with my choosing to list exactly 18 signs of the times pertinent to an Antichrist in election 2024.

CHAPTER EIGHT

HILDEGARD OF BINGEN: THE ANTICHRIST AS PATRIARCHY

We saw in chapter three how Hildegard of Bingen painted the Christ as a Healing Christ and Blue Man to be found in all of us.

In a particularly vivid illustration of evil, Antichrist, and the battle against powers and principalities, Hildegard — recently formally declared a saint and doctor of the church — painted a picture of what she calls the "Antichrist." We reproduce her painting in this book (see page 50). It borrows heavily from the Book of the Apocalypse and her sense of the End Times. In it, she pictures evil and the coming of chaos as the unraveling of the ropes of justice that keep order to society. (Recall that in her painting of the "Blue Man" golden ropes stand for God the Creator as well as for the ropes that keep creation together). The Antichrist seeks to undo that sense of order in favor of unvarnished chaos.

The beasts in her painting are accomplishing this unraveling of order by pulling on a rope. Among them are, in her words, "a fiery dog that was not burning; a lion that was reddish-brown; a pale horse; a black pig; and a grisly wolf." Each was pulling hard on a piece of rope in his mouth and the rope symbolized the binding that holds together an interdependent and compassionate universe. Each was doing its part to bring on chaos, the unraveling of cosmic order. What does each beast stand for?

The fiery dog stands for humans who "bite at their own condition" and who do not burn with justice. The reddish lion stands for "warlike men" who wage wars without considering God's judgment. The pale horse stands for those who put luxury living and their own selfish pleasure before the performance of worthwhile acts. The black pig stands for rulers who create sadness and uncleanness in themselves and their subjects. The wolf stands for those who rob others. The black rope, she tells us, represents "the darkness that stretches out many injustices."

She pictures Christ as a young man, "the Son of Man who is the beginning of justice who watches over the strength of the union of mirror knowledge and human work." Mirror knowledge being the truth that humans are images of God (*Tselem*) and can act like it. We can be both just and compassionate to self and others. Like Signorelli who came three centuries after her, Hildegard also pictures Enoch and Elijah as witnesses who lead the people back from Satan. Elijah is a symbol of the prophets and stands for John the Baptist who was a prophetic precursor of Christ. Such prophets "carry the banner of the justice of God and put the devil to flight." The demonic forces will yield to Christ who is "a very strong warrior" and will "break the head of injustice." Justice and beauty will triumph.

Hildegard paints an ugly head breaking loose from a mother figure and the head is topped with human dung. "A monstrous and very black head appeared, having fiery eyes and ears like the ears of an ass and nostrils and mouth like the nostrils and mouth of a lion, crunching with a great jaw and cutting horribly like horrible iron teeth." Moving with "monstrous ugliness, it spreads a foul odor on the mountain" and "tears the institutions of the church to pieces with the crudest greediness" and causes bloody wounds on the thighs of the mother figure. Who is this figure?

It is "the Antichrist, the son of injustice, the cursed one of the cursed ones." With it, death rushes into the church and this happens "because faith staggers in people and the Gospel limps in some people… The divine Scriptures have been rendered lukewarm."

Hildegard addresses the monster: "O you cave of injustice… your works seek the pit of hell. You will live absorbed in your gluttony there and that hellish place will vomit forth stink. The world will recognize in this stench the bitterness of death in the destroyer of destructions."

Hildegard paints an exaggerated and aggressive penis in this same picture which to me signifies the toxic masculine of a one-sided and dominating patriarchy that Hildegard is sensing in her unconscious.

The monster who she names the "worst of beasts" joins up with kings, dukes, leaders, and those with money and prestige. It sounds like a presidential election. He steals land, destroys insight, and covers up the powers of the inner person to see truth. This "devil has no power in good things, but only in evil things of eternal death."

Hildegard is naming how our personal faults such as lying and greed and indifference to justice can feed societal sins and crush humanity's promise, destroy institutions such as the church, and taint human history. Elections have consequences and our choices and elections have consequences that spread far beyond our own private sphere. Our interconnectivity applies to the sharing of grace and joy, but also to the sharing of rupture and evil. In this blunt and shocking painting, Hildegard paints a powerful picture of the Antichrist that rivals Signorelli's in its fury and naming of the Antichrist, the "worst of beasts."

CONCLUSION

BE A CAMEL AND ESCAPE THE ALLUREMENT OF THE ANTICHRIST

We have spoken of the Antichrist as a powerful archetype and its corresponding opposite archetype as Christ, the incarnation of love, justice and compassion. We have considered Signorelli's and Hildegard's effort to tell the Antichrist story in imagery. Weber summarizes the impact from Signorelli's painting of the Antichrist when he says that "the scenes in the Capella Nova are as brave in their way as Picasso's *Guernica* was in the light of Franco's evils." I think the same might be said of Hildegard's bravery. It is the artist's gift to remind us of the depths of goodness and the depths of evil that humanity carries within us.

Jung did not see archetypes as "inherited ideas," but as "inherited, instinctive impulses and forms" and "patterns of behavior." In calling a contemporary political leader and movement the "Antichrist" we are recognizing the power behind the instinctive impulses and patterns of behavior it elicits. All archetypes carry a polarity, hot and cold, short and tall, the Good-Christ vs. evil-Antichrist. "The Antichrist develops in legend as a perverse imitator of Christ's life.

He is… an imitating spirit of evil who follows in Christ's footsteps like a shadow following the body."

Jungian teacher Sue Mehrtens, in a thoughtful article on Jung and the Antichrist archetype recounts how Jung warned that archetypes hold a "seductive quality that lies in their numinosity." It "seizes hold of the individual in a startling way, creating a condition amounting almost to possession, the consequences of which may be incalculable." Mehrtens comments that throughout human history Antichrists have appeared with the power to "stir up the crowd, encourage 'mass-mindedness' (which Jung regards as dangerous and dehumanizing), and sway their followers to commit atrocities in the name of tribe, country or God."

We therefore must become more aware and conscious, so we don't fall into this seduction by failing to apply our critical faculties to what we see happening all around us. In other words, we must beware of lies and falsehoods and misinformation and hypocrisy and cover up. We must seek out truth and the sources of truth and resist propaganda and those who use lies as a weapon to sow chaos on a regular basis. We must think for ourselves. We must "come to terms drastically with the facts as they are, with the absolute opposition that is not tearing the world asunder politically but has planted a schism in the human heart."

Mehrtens also proposes that both Donald Trump and Vladimir Putin are named by the Antichrist archetype today. The Antichrist "is someone who foments division, encourages violence, abuses people, lies, creates chaos, and contravenes norms of decency." He is also one who fascinates. Sadly, much media and social media today are powered by algorithms of that which fascinates. That is a very dangerous situation for a culture to find itself in. Lying and disinformation today can readily tear the world asunder politically.

CONCLUSION

There can be no community without a quest for facts and truths we can share in common. Lies will tear communities apart from the inside out, from the heart out, indeed from a "schism in the human heart."

Another admonition in resisting the Antichrist according to Jung and Mehrtens is to stay "grounded, rooted, practical, and resist 'spacing out.'" And resist "psychic epidemics" such as Q-anon nonsense and lots of darkness emanating from current right-wing politicos about how we live in a dark America altogether, a dystopian vision such as Donald Trump painted on the day of his inauguration in 2016 and continues to talk about to this day. We named in chapter six how American history holds a darkness, a grotesqueness to it. All of human history has its grotesque stories to tell—from cannibalism to wars to pogroms and the rest. That is why truth is so important and guarding our hearts both individually and collectively is so important. *America is not only its grotesqueness.*

It is also its considerable achievements in offering a promise that "all men (meaning all people) are created equal." And in spreading that promise and, thanks to protest and action and through fits and starts has evolved to live up to that promise more fully for it is a big promise that does not come easily. And offering it as an aspiration and a light on a pedestal. In welcoming refugees from many countries relief and opportunities, it holds up a lamp as the statue of liberty did to those millions who migrated to America for good reason. Recall words from the sonnet written on the occasion of the inauguration of that statue:

"A mighty woman with a torch, whose flame / is the imprisoned lightning, and her name / Mother of Exiles. From her beacon-hand /glows world-wide welcome... / Give me your tired, your poor /

your huddled masses yearning to breathe free / the wretched refuse of your teeming shore. / Send these, the homeless, tempest-tost to me / I lift my lamp beside the golden door!"

It is telling that a woman wrote this poem. Emma Lazarus welcomes immigrants with a *Lady* of Liberty. The promise is a maternal one, a promise of compassion. Lazarus calls it "The New Colossus" in contrast to the Colossus of Rhodes, one of the Seven Wonders of the ancient world. She contrasts that ancient symbol of the 3rd century BC—"the brazen giant of Greek fame"—with a "New" Colossus—the Statue of Liberty, "a female embodiment of commanding maternal strength and 'Mother of Exiles.'" The light in the torch –"imprisoned lightning"—was, in 1883, electricity—a new and exciting technology. Lazarus was an activist and advocate for Jewish refugees fleeing persecution in Imperial Russia. The poem turned "Liberty into a welcoming mother, a symbol of hope to the outcasts and downtrodden of the world," comments one observer. Julian of Norwich, who wrote about compassion being at the heart of motherliness, would be pleased. So too would Hildegard, who sang how a young woman named Love was the "source of this creation" and "the whole of creation calls this maiden 'Lady.'" The return of the feminine, the divine mother, happens.

America still has a feminine soul to her. A caring and compassionate soul. And that is the promise. Not hate. Not power for power's sake. Not patriarchy seeking revenge and retribution. Not attacks on women's bodies from politicians abetted by religious figures. Not "justice" that serves corporations and the superrich. But justice that serves the poor. Like Mary stood for in the Middle Ages as Henry Adams points out. Not the reptilian brain unleashed but a caring heart that is godlike and that Jesus taught: "Be you compassionate as your Father in heaven is compassionate" (Lk

6:36). And that the Dalai Lama calls "my religion." And that Judaism calls "the secret name of God." And that Muhammed names in the Koran when talking frequently of "Allah, the compassionate one." This is the Christ in America 2024. And it contrasts ever so sharply with the Antichrist of 2024 wherever it is at work with all of its dark money and secret deeds of hate and division.

Jung also recommends keeping one's distance from mobs and mass gatherings and resisting 'group think' and 'mass-mindedness.' We need to be aware of the Antichrist's "tendency to divide" and "its lust for power." There is a reason the Antichrist is called the "prince of this world."

Because we do possess the "spirit of truth who has taken up his abode in man," we can and need to discern truth from falsity and truth from 'fake news' and disinformation. We must question authority and find its locus within ourselves. And we must recognize the Antichrist for what it is: dangerous, and, as Jung warns, 'the less he is recognized the more dangerous he is.'" Thus the reason for this book—to render the Antichrist visible among us so we can talk about it and not be isolated. We are stronger in community. And we are called to resist.

Above all, says Jung, we need to "find our way back to the original living spirit which is also a mediator and uniter of opposites." I think the mystics help us especially in this sacred return. Psychologist Otto Rank, like Jung a pupil of Freud who eventually parted ways with him, talks about humans holding an "original wound" that can only be healed by the *"unio mystica,"* the mystical union which, he believes, we undergo by way of "love and art." Spirituality is found in nature, "the epitome of the irrational is the marvel of creation itself." Meister Eckhart too talks about beauty as "salvation."

We are invited to find the mystic in ourselves, the lover of life who has taken heed of the *oneings* (Julian of Norwich's term) and *ecstasies* (Thomas Aquinas's term) and *breakthroughs* (Meister Eckhart's term)—the experiences of the divine that have come our way. To me this means recovering the Via Positiva—our love of life—a profound sense of biophilia, the joy and gratitude for living. To battle necrophilia, we must at dark times that seem like end times like ours become like camels who fill up at oases of biophilia and joy as we travel what is often a dry and demanding desert. We can then, as Jung tells us, "commit to being a force for unification and reconciliation." Meister Eckhart teaches, "isness is God" and "if the only prayer you say in your whole life is 'Thank you,' that would suffice." All that is biophilia. Psychologist Erich Fromm warns us that "necrophilia grows when biophilia is stunted." The Antichrist is a champion of necrophilia. Christ champions biophilia. "I come that you may have life and have it in abundance" (Jn 10:10).

Thus we can call on the "strength of the positive pole of the archetype. The Antichrist would destroy—we can build. The Antichrist would lie—we can speak the truth. The Antichrist projects the shadow and labels other people and groups of people as evil ("venom" in Trump's words)—we can choose to internalize the shadow by looking within and facing our own inner failings. Said Jung in a 1940 letter during the Nazi times. "There is only one certainty—nothing can put out the light within."

This echoes the teaching from Meister Eckhart that the spark of the soul that burns in all of us can never be extinguished. The Antichrist does not have the last word. The Word that comes in the deep silence and in the silence that awe makes has the last word.

The title of Hildegard of Bingen's first book was: *Scivias*, "Know the ways," meaning know the ways of *folly* vs. the ways of *wisdom*.

CONCLUSION

Know and choose. Humanity is in such a place today collectively. The ways of Christ are wise, the ways of the Antichrist are folly. Ignoring climate change and the plight of Mother Earth is pure folly. Carrying on wars is pure folly. Humanity must move from folly to wisdom before it is too late. We are assisted clearly by Webb Telescope and the pictures from Voyager One that remind us what a special and unique planet we dwell on in this vast universe of two trillion galaxies, each with hundreds of billions of stars.

Can humanity abandon our compulsions to dominate one another militarily and instead join forces to push back against climate change? In this way we would fulfill the promise of the Scriptures: "This is wisdom, to love life" (Ecclesiasticus 4:13). Biophilia—for ourselves and our descendants and Mother Earth herself with all her beautiful creatures—would follow. It is significant that the alternative to Trump and MAGA this election is a woman, Kamala Harris, and a woman of color. Joy abounds at this possibility in the hearts of many, myself included. The Dalai Lama proposed several years ago that "Western women will save the world." Was he right?

EPILOGUE

CHRIST, ANTICHRIST, AND THE 2024 ELECTION

Christ represents the best in humanity—what Abraham Lincoln called "our better angels." The archetype of the Antichrist stands for what is worst in humanity, what is portrayed in Signorelli's fresco as the devil whispering in the ear of the Antichrist who is, in his narcissism, pointing at himself.

The Christ represents light and peace and truth and life and biophilia. Love of nature and earth and justice therefore and our capacities for healing and forgiveness and compassion and joy and celebration. One whose first miracle was to bring more wine to a wedding feast and who declares he had come "to bring life in abundance."

Dignity of the individual and the community and therefore government of, by and for the people are central to this worldview.

The Antichrist represents narcissism and anger and retaliation and revenge. And division and chaos and denial of the suffering of others including Mother Earth and the destruction that climate change can and is bringing about. The Antichrist stands for lying and patriarchy and the reptilian brain unleashed—power over, not power with. Not democracy but government of the few, by the few, and for the few that serves the few and denies the dignity of the many.

Looking again at the Antichrist in the Orvieto Cathedral, we can recognize the following elements in the fresco. According to commentators on the frescos, the Antichrist is a "tyrant" with "totalitarian power" and a "totalitarian society" is his goal. He is the "emissary" of Satan who takes on the "appearance of the Messiah." He "deceives men and gains their consent" while promoting himself "as an enlightened leader and guide." But "in reality he is simply the animated puppet used by Satan to carry out his plan."

In Signorelli's fresco, the Antichrist stands on a pedestal with features that resemble Christ. Yet "his gaze appears sinister and disturbing, his eyes crossed. The curls of his hair suggest horns," and his left arm merges with that of the demon whispering in his ear. He is working arm in arm with the demon. His right arm points to himself "as though proclaiming himself God and calling men to follow him (Thess 2:4)." Through lies and charm and false appearances, he will convince "many to become his disciples."

The choice is ours in election 2024. It always has been. *Electio* is Latin for choice. From that word we get the word, *election*.

What shall we choose?

AFTERWORD

by Andrew Harvey

"*Love is victorious. Amen.*" These are the last words of Thomas Merton's final lecture. Of all the great and pioneering works Matthew Fox has graced us with over five decades of prophetic creativity as our greatest living Christian theologian, this may be the most important. It is certainly the bravest, the riskiest, and the most affronting to anyone who doubts the existence and terrible power of evil in our expanding global dark night. Matthew Fox has always risen to name and call out evil in all forms; now in his early 80s he names and calls out, with a clarity and sober but bladed vehemence of heart, evil at its source and in its most devastating embodiment to warn us and to prepare us for the inner and outer struggles we must shoulder to preserve our world against the unprecedented constellation of dark forces that now nakedly menace its survival.

Many mystic teachers and contemplatives I know have begun to see the truth of what Matt has laid out so masterfully and plainly for us. Once again, he has stepped out first alone to tell us what he sees and knows to be real, without fear of derision or consequences, and to model to all of us what sacred integrity demands. In an age of canny marketing and branding, Matt is modeling what it is to accept and bear to the end a prophetic destiny, come what may.

Gratitude for his spiritual heroism is not enough. We all must catch fire from it immediately if we are truly to both grasp and incarnate the implications of his analysis. An Antichrist of enormous and horrifying dark power has emerged in the squalid, psychopathic, fathomlessly corrupt person of a master-manipulator of all our worst emotions, most destructive fears, most embedded prejudices and most lethal addictions to power and money and the dark passion to live free from any responsibility to the abandoned and marginalized and to Nature herself. The plan of the Antichrist is to rubble the divine image in humanity and to inaugurate a worldwide authoritarian empire of lies and cruelty that has been exposed in Project 2025. Donald Trump's nihilistic depravity, incapacity to tell the truth, insatiable appetite for dominance and the dreadful charisma he emanates that has blinded, vampirized and infantilized millions make him its ordained and perfect executant. To underestimate the power that is using him, protecting him, guiding him invites catastrophe; the rise of a uniquely American fascism, the demonic Christofascism that Matt eviscerates with such chiseled outrage will be unprecedented danger not only to the American adventure of democracy, but to the future of humanity itself. Anyone who sees that clearly now needs to pray for the grace to bear what they see without dying of fear and heartbreak and to work humbly, calmly and with relentless focus on the Light in every inner and outer realm to prevent this disaster that could drastically accelerate the annihilation of humanity and a massive part of Nature.

Like Matt, I believe that humanity can and will raggedly rise to this challenge and everything I have written and done in these last decades has been dedicated to making its terms as clear as I can to be of the most help.

AFTERWORD

Of all the great mystical traditions, the authentic Christian mystical tradition of which Matthew Fox is our living elder statesman has the starkest and most realistic awareness of evil, a realism all the other traditions would be wise to integrate immediately. Those, who in the face of what is everywhere erupting, claim that evil does not exist or that it is either "ignorance" or "illusion" or that we must pay no attention to it because attention feeds it, collude in the blindness and cowardice on which its quantum explosion feeds.

There is one more essential treasure, however, that Jesus and the Christian mystics offer us that I believe we all need to integrate at the richest depth we are capable of. This is the astounding realization, grounded directly in the miracle of the Resurrection, that terrifying though evil is, and terrible though the Antichrist is with all its systems of cold cruelty now in place, there is a far greater power of Eternal Light that uses without them knowing, both evil and its emissary, the Antichrist for the Divine's own magical and redemptive purposes. By the light of this revelation, we can begin to see that the sign of the rise of the Antichrist is a sign, too, of the coming birth of a new creation and the new divine human. The ancient alchemists knew that the greatest light is born from the greatest darkness. The crucifixion of the Christ by the Antichrist forces of his time did not only not destroy the truth of his sublime mission, it proved to be against all reason or conceivable precedent, the childbed of the Resurrection. Our global dark night is taking humanity to the cross; the Antichrist has prepared his horrible Golgotha—the mesmerized MAGA minions and their authoritarian brothers and sisters all over the world are assembling and hissing. They may seem to win for a time and devastatingly, but they cannot. The arc of history the Christ has shown us, bends not only towards justice but to resurrection.

Let all of us who with Matthew Fox's help can now see the dangers clearly also see clearly that they presage an unimaginable Birth for which we must now be prepared to give, endure, and hope everything. "*O da quod iubes Domine*," wrote St. Augustine. Oh Lord, give what you demand.

And He will. In fact, He already has.

APPENDIX

MAGA'S PRECARIOUS MANHOOD VS. AUTHENTIC MASCULINITY

by Matthew Fox

As we saw in chapter eight, Hildegard names and paints Patriarchy as Antichrist in a most vivid manner — quite stunning for a saint and doctor of the church.

In an article following the Republican convention this summer, Harold Meyerson talks about the Republican party as a "party of precarious manhood." He cites Donald Trump's admiration of Hungary's Victor Orban, lauding him as "a very tough man" and records Trump's pleasure when Orban said of him, "everybody was afraid of him." Trump admires strongmen such as Putin and North Korea's Kim Jong Un for their toughness.

The MAGA movement is "reliant on the cult of toughness and hypermasculinity," Meyerson believes, because it has delivered nothing that is tangible to address the loss of good blue-collar jobs especially in the Midwest. In contrast, the infrastructure bill and the Inflation Reduction Act under Biden "have led to the first major increase in factory construction in several decades." That plus union-scale wages have returned on Biden's watch. Meyerson sees the violent rhetoric in MAGA as a compensation for Trump delivering nothing when he was president — and "violent rhetoric is Trump's mother tongue."

One of the invited speakers at the Republican convention was entertainer and wrestler Hulk Hogan who put on a brief talk that included working mightily to rip off his shirt. Also featured was Dana White, president of UFC, Ultimate Fighting Championship. Clearly, it was an effort to feature the "real men" who are "real Americans" (a term repeated frequently by Hulk Hogan in his remarks).

Right on cue, Hulk Hogan threatened to "body-slam" Kamala Harris and made a racist comment her at a public bar on the first night of the Democratic Convention in Chicago. A masculinity issue indeed.

That masculinity is in a state of flux—and ought to be, given the damage and excesses Patriarchy has wrought over the last thousands of years—is no secret. It is why I wrote my book sixteen years ago, *The Hidden Spirituality of Men: Ten Metaphors to Awaken the Sacred Masculine.* But whether a MAGA definition of masculinity is the way to go is very problematic. As David French put it in an article entitled "Hulk Hogan Is Not the Only Way to Be a Man," there is "a seductive quality to Trump's masculinity. Grievance is a form of counterfeit purpose, and anger is a form of counterfeit courage." Grievance leads to "fighting the hated foe," but "when you center masculinity on grievance and anger rather than honor and courage, you attract men like Hogan and Kid Rock," but you leave a lot out. In my words, you bring forth the reptilian brain in spades, but ignore the mammal brain where compassion reigns.

APPENDIX

David French holds up a commencement speech delivered by Admiral William McRaven, former Navy Seal and designer of the team who killed Osama bin Laden, who told the college graduates: "You must have compassion. You must ache for the poor and disenfranchised. You must feel for the vulnerable. You must weep for the ill and infirm. You must pray for those who are without hope. You must be kind to those less fortunate." Said French, "That's the message American men need to hear. That's a message the American people need to hear." Citing JD Vance, the vice-presidential candidate to Donald Trump, who says "our people hate the right people," French observes, "that's the language of grievance and anger. But there's a better way for men—for all of us. It's rooted in honor, courage and love."

I find a new and healthier masculinity in my exploration of ten archetypes fit for our times. They are quite opposite to the MAGA approach of grievance and anger and power-over. The Antichrist offers a faux version of masculinity. Fascism in all its incarnations constitutes a faux version of masculinity and is incompatible with the Christ. It is the opposite, a sign of the Antichrist. I name seven of the ten healthy masculine archetypes briefly here.

1) Father Sky—to recognize the vastness of the universe to which we belong is to move well beyond narcissism or the big "I" to something much larger than ourselves—that which has made us rather than what we make.
2) The Green Man is an archetype that connects us to the vegetative world, to roots and trees and interdependence with the earth and inspires us to be warriors defending Mother Earth. This is in contrast to proposing that if fossil

fuel captains offer me one billion dollars, I will set all laws protecting her on fire (which Trump proposed).

3) The Spiritual warrior uses one's inner strength to wage battle on behalf of values that matter and feed the common good—of which saving Mother Earth is one solid example.

4) The Blue Man archetype is, as Hildegard paints it on page 49 of this book, an archetype that names our powers of healing and compassion and creativity and how we all carry a healing Christ within us. Healing, not dividing. Healing, not hoarding or name-calling and projecting.

5) The Father archetype invites forward a man's capacities for caring for others and protecting the young and vulnerable. Often when men become fathers, they grow up fast and learn to take responsibility for persons other than oneself.

6) The hunter-gatherer archetype recognizes how we all carry within us that inherited DNA from our ancestors that focused on hunting and on gathering, on going out of ourselves to find truth and find wisdom and grow our minds as well as our hearts. And this for the sake of the greater whole, the tribe.

7) The grandfather archetype is that of the elder whose job it is to share stories with the younger generation and to display one's gratitude for life and the beauty bestowed on others. It is also a time for letting go and not clinging and thinking of the coming generations. A time for wisdom and encouraging the young in their healthy pursuits to live and love fully and to save the planet for future generations.

To move beyond Patriarchy is to move to a world where caring is more a value than scaring; love than fear; joy than hatred; peace than war. This move begins in the human heart but does not stay there: it moves into society and reaches into politics.

Perhaps it is becoming incarnated at this moment in the person of a potentially first woman president in Kamala Harris who carries the energy of a strong and accomplished woman and in her running mate, Tim Walz. The former can represent the strong feminine such as the Black Madonna incarnates who puts justice for the poor and disenfranchised first, and who marries joy and justice in her manner and message. And the latter can represent the healthy masculine, for his track record in politics is not one of shaming and grievance and anger, but of working with others out of a caring for others. Good teachers and coaches and congress people and governors develop the habits and virtues that bring about such transformation. Joy follows from a commitment to such values. And joy is contagious as well as energizing.

ENDNOTES

The opening quotes by Thomas Aquinas can be found in Matthew Fox, *Sheer Joy: Conversations with Thomas Aquinas on Creation Spirituality*, Ixia Press, 2020, p. 162, pp. 471f., and p. 493.

INTRODUCTION:
An "Aha!" Moment in a Church in Orvieto

p. xviii Information about Luther and his connection to Valla can be found here: https://www.cambridge.org/core/journals/renaissance-quarterly/article/abs/papal-antichrist-martin-luther-and-the-underappreciated-influence-of-lorenzo-valla/E1F49EC158698145BC3CAA01ABC31BD1

pp. xvi-xvii "dancing their hideous dance" … "like a bomb" … quotes from Nicholas Fox Weber, *Freud's Trip to Orvieto: The Great Doctor's Unresolved Confrontation with Antisemitism, Death, and Homoeroticism; His Passion for Paintings; and the Writer in His Footsteps,* Bellevue Literary Press, 2017, pp. 85, 76.

CHAPTER 1
Freud's Encounter with the Antichrist Painting in Orvieto Cathedral

p. 1 "The finest paintings I have ever seen." These words by Freud as quoted in Leanne Ogasawara, "When Freud Met the Antichrist in Orvieto" https://3quarksdaily.com/3quarksdaily/2020/06/when-freud-met-the-antichrist-in-orvieto.html

pp. 1-2 Quotes from Weber found in *Freud's Trip to Orvieto*, pp. 15, 28, 59, 73.

p. 2 "one of the highest examples of Italian painting" quote from Giuseppe Mearilli, *Orvieto Duomo: Cathedral of the Assumption*, Perugia: Quattroemme, 2013, p. 39. Mearilli also describes Signorelli as "a realist, an innovator, a forerunner of 16th century art" on p. 77.

p. 3 "With the world entering a new half millennium… a new immediacy." Quote from Weber in *Freud's Trip to Orvieto*, p. 150.

p. 3 Quotes from Edward F. Edinger, *Apocalypse: A Jungian Study of the Book of Revelation*, Chicago: Open Court, 1999, p. 5.

pp. 4f. All the Freudian quotes are found in Kendra Cherry, MSEd, "Sigmund Freud on Religion: The Perspective of a Jewish atheist scientist," https://www.verywellmind.com/freud-religion-2795858

pp. 5-7 "one of the significant pilgrimages of his life… " and following quotes from N. Weber are found in his *Freud's Trip to Orvieto*, pp. 92f., 312, 229, 11, 26-28, 180f, 135, 104f.

p. 7 "the most important event, the most poignant loss, of a man's life." This quote from Freud is found in Weber, *Freud's Trip to Orvieto*, at p. 31.

CHAPTER 2
The Antichrist as a Naming of Evil

Matthew Fox, *Sins of the Spirit, Blessings of the Flesh: Transforming Evil in Soul and Society,* Berkeley, Ca.: North Atlantic Books, 2016.

CHAPTER 3
Christ as Archetype

p. 13 Nancy E. Abrams, *A God That Could be Real: Spirituality, Science and the Future of Our Planet,* Boston: Beacon Press, 2016.

p. 13 David M. Seidenberg, *Kabbalah and Ecology: God's Image in More-Than-Human World,* Cambridge University Press, 2015.

p. 14 The Zohar quotes are found in Matthew Fox, *One River, Many Wells: Wisdom Springing From Global Faiths,* Penguin Books 2014, pp. 63-67.

p. 15 The Gospel of Thomas quote is found in Fox, *One River, Many Wells,* p. 67.

pp. 15-16 The Hildegard quotes are found in Fox, *One River, Many Wells,* pp. 70f.

p. 16 The Mechtild of Magdeburg and the Meister Eckhart quotes are found in Fox, *One River, Many Wells,* p. 72.

pp. 16-17 The Thomas Aquinas quotes are found in Fox, *One River, Many Wells,* p. 69.

p. 17 The Egyptian wisdom quote is found in Fox, *One River, Many Wells,* p. 55.

pp. 17-18 The Celtic quotes are found in Fox, *One River, Many Wells,* p. 56.

p. 18 The Baghavad Gita quotes are found in Fox, *One River, Many Wells,* p. 61.

pp. 20f. The Meister Eckhart quotes are found in Fox, *Passion for Creation: the Earth-Honoring Spirituality of Meister Eckhart,* Inner Traditions, 2000, pp. 311, 384, 322, 330.

p. 22 For the "blue man" see "Chapter 8: The Blue Man" in Matthew Fox, *The Hidden Spirituality of Men: Ten Metaphors to Awaken the Sacred Masculine,* New World Library, 2009, pp. 153-172.

p. 22 The Hildegard quotes are found in Matthew Fox, *Illuminations of Hildegard of Bingen,* Bear&Co., 2003, pp. 34f.

CHAPTER 4
The Antichrist as Archetype

p. 23 Steven B. Herrmann, "Notes on Meister Eckhart's Trial and Defense: The Archetype of Anti-Christ in 1328." Unpublished paper shared with Matthew Fox, July, 2024, p. 1. See also, Steven B. Herrmann, *Meister Eckhart and C. G. Jung On the Vocation of the Self,* Bloomington, Ind.: iUniverse, 2024.

p. 23 The Edinger's quote is found in his book *Apocalypse,* p. 5.

pp. 24-25 "could be considered the most perfect model..." is a quote from Weber, *Freud's Trip,* p. 90. Next quote from Weber on the same page.

pp. 25-26 "The tyrant points to his own head..." "...everyone will have to decide which side to take..." "He will be a crowd-pleaser..." "...in reality he is nothing other than a master of deceit..." "...will end up exchanging good for evil and evil for good..." "...the two will face each other..." are quotes from Fabio Massimo Del Sole and Patrizia Pelorosso in *The Duomo of Orvieto and the Apocalypse of Luca Signorelli,* Orvieto: Mirabilia, 2023, pp. 69, 62, 68, 70.

pp. 26-27 Some of the description of Signorelli's fresco is derived from Mearilli, *Orvieto Duomo,* pp. 76ff.

ENDNOTES

p. 27 The quote from Aquinas, "A politician must know more about the human soul..." is found in Fox, *Sheer Joy*, p. 394.

p. 27 For Ogasawara, see note above in chapter one.

p. 28 The quote from Aquinas, "The proper objects of the heart..." is found in Fox, *Sheer Joy*, p. 289.

CHAPTER 5
Jesus and Democracy

The quotes by Thomas Aquinas can be found in Fox, *Sheer Joy*, p. 162, p. 471.

p. 31f. For Eckhart and all Eckhart quotes in this chapter, see "Sermon Thirty-six: Everyone an Aristocrat, Everyone a Royal Person," in Fox, *Passion for Creation*, pp. 510-530.

p. 32 See Helen A. Kenik, "Toward a Biblical Basis for Creation Theology," in Matthew Fox (ed.), *Western Spirituality: Historical Roots, Ecumenical Routes*, Bear & Co., 1987, pp. 27-75.

CHAPTER 6
MAGA: Making America Grotesque Again

p. 51 on the "Middle Passage" https://www.statista.com/statistics/1143458/annual-share-slaves-deaths-during-middle-passage/

p. 51 on the Civil War https://www.bbc.com/news/magazine-17604991

CHAPTER 7
18 Signs of the Times: The Antichrist in American Politics, 2024

p. 59 On point 2: civicshout.com July 7

p. 61 On point 5: Regulations are the means by which… practical guardrails" quote from Robert Reich, *The Six Corporate-Owned Supreme Court Justices Have Completed Their Assigned Mission* at https://www.commondreams.org/opinion/powell-memo-supreme-court

pp. 62f. On point 6: Facts reported in this point can be checked in Reich's article above.

pp. 63f. On point 6: Information and quotes about the Heritage Foundation found in the article by Mark Sumner, *Meet the Group Behind Trump's Fascist 2025 Agenda* at https://www.dailykos.com/stories/2024/7/7/2251083/-Meet-the-group-behind-Trump-s-fascist-2025-agenda; information and quotes about the Opus Dei issue are found in the article by Rachel Leingang and Stephanie Kirchgaessner, *Kevin Roberts, architect of Project 2025, has close ties to radical Catholic group Opus Dei* https://www.theguardian.com/us-news/article/2024/jul/26/kevin-roberts-project-2025-opus-dei

p. 64 Sheldon Whitehouse's quotes in point 7 are found in the article by Meteor Blades, *Sen. Sheldon Whitehouse Tells It Like It Is: One Crew, One Plan, One Cancer in the Body Politic* at https://www.dailykos.com/stories/2024/7/2/2250607/-Sen-Sheldon-Whitehouse-tells-it-like-it-is-one-crew-one-plan-one-cancer-in-the-body-politic

pp. 65-66 Quotes in point 8 are from this article by Robert L. Borosage, *Why Trump's Second Victory Would Be Worse* at https://www.thenation.com/article/society/project-2025-trump-heritage-foundation-maga/

p. 67 For the Kevin Roberts' quote, see this report from Associated Press: https://www.politico.com/news/2024/07/04/leader-of-the-pro-trump-project-2025-suggests-there-will-be-a-new-american-revolution-00166583

p. 67 The petition can be found here: https://civicshout.com/p/fire-heritage-foundation-president-for-violent-rhetoric?

ENDNOTES

p. 68 The Bannon quote in point 11 can be found here https://www.snopes.com/fact-check/bannon-hell-capitol-attack/

p. 70 The quote from José Miranda in point 13 is found in Matthew Fox, *Original Blessing: A Primer in Creation Spirituality*, Tarcher/Penguin, 2000, p. 287.

p. 71 For "compassion means justice" see Fox, *Passion for Creation*, pp. 467ff.

pp. 71-73 Information and quotes for point 14 are found in Robert L. Borosage, *Why Trump's Second Victory Would Be Worse* (see link above).

p. 73 "MAGA imperial presidency... is equal parts Cotton Mather and Roy Cohn" quote found in Chris Lehmann, *The Theocratic Blueprint for Trump's Next Term* here https://www.thenation.com/article/society/russell-vought-center-renewing-america-christian-nationalism/

p. 74 The quotes "It's a christofascist's wish list... and bigotry" and "a remarkably detailed guide... into a fascist's paradise" for in point 15 can be found at https://newrepublic.com/post/183557/project-2025-hate-groups-advisers-trump

p. 76 The Thomas Aquinas quote is from his treatise *On Evil*, q. 12, art. 4.

p. 77 The Thomas Aquinas quote is cited in Fox, *Sheer Joy*, p. 417.

p. 77 The Coppins quotes can be found in the article by Taeggad Goddard, *A Close Reading of the prayers at Trump Rallies* https://politicalwire.com/2024/07/29/a-close-reading-of-the-prayers-at-a-trump-rally/

p. 78 The Robert P. Jones quote in point 18 can be found here in Thomas Edsall, *The Deification of Donald Trump Poses Some Interesting Questions*, see https://www.nytimes.com/2024/01/17/opinion/trump-god-evangelicals-anointed.html

p. 78 The Kimberly Vaughn quote and other information cited in point 18 about Trump rallies can be read in Peter Smith, *God, Guns & Trump: Jesus is their savior, Trump is their candidate*, Montreal Gazette, May

18, 2024 https://montrealgazette.com/news/world/god-guns-trump-jesus-is-their-savior-donald-trump-is-their-president

p. 78 For the "God Bless the USA Bible" see https://www.thedailybeast.com/donald-trump-made-dollar300k-endorsing-bible

p.78 The quote from Jim Guth and other information cited in point 18, including the quote by Eric Trump, can be found in Thomas Edsall, *The Deification of Donald Trump* (see above).

CHAPTER 8
Hildegard of Bingen: The Antichrist as Patriarchy

Quotes from Hildegard are found in Matthew Fox, *Illuminations of Hildegard of Bingen,* Bear&Co., 2003, p. 123f.

CONCLUSION
Be a Camel and Escape the Allurement of the Antichrist

p. 85 Weber's quote in his *Freud's Trip to Orvieto,* p. 207.

pp. 85-90 "The Antichrist develops in legend…" is a quote taken from Sue Mehrtens' essay *Understanding What We Are Dealing With: Jung on the Antichrist Archetype* found here: https://jungiancenter.org/understanding-what-were-dealing-with-jung-on-the-antichrist-archetype/. All the other quotes in this Conclusion by Mehrtens and by Jung can be found in the same essay.

pp. 87-88 One can read Lazarus' sonnet here: https://en.wikipedia.org/wiki/The_New_Colossus

p. 88 For the reference to Julian of Norwich, see Matthew Fox, *Julian of Norwich: Wisdom in a Time of Pandemic—and Beyond*, iUniverse, 2020, pp. 45-58.

ENDNOTES

p. 88 The quotes from Hildegard can be found in Matthew Fox, *Hildegard of Bingen, a Saint For Our Times*, Namaste, 2012, p. xiii.

p. 88 For the Henry Adams reference, see R. P. Blackmur, "The Virgin and the Dynamo," in *Henry Adams*, New York: Harcourt Brace Jovanovich, 1980, pp. 202-209.

p. 89 For the quotes about Otto Rank, see Matthew Fox, "Psychotherapy and the 'Unio Mystica': Meister Eckhart Meets Otto Rank," in Matthew Fox, *Meister Eckhart: A Mystic-Warrior for Our Times*, Novato: New World Library, 2014, pp. 139-156.

p. 90 For the Meister Eckhart quotes, see Matthew Fox, *Meditations with Meister Eckhart*, Inner Traditions/Bear, 1983, pp. 12, 34.

p. 90 The quote from Jung "There is only one certainty… the light within" is found in "Letter to Mary Mellon," 19 June 1940.

EPILOGUE

p. 94 The descriptive quotes of Signorelli's fresco in this section are found in Fabio M. Del Sole and Patrizia Pelorosso in *The Duomo of Orvieto and the Apocalypse of Luca Signorelli*, pp. 69, 62, and 59.

APPENDIX

The book on masculinity referenced in this section is Matthew Fox, *The Hidden Spirituality of Men: Ten Metaphors to Awaken the Sacred Masculine*, New World Library, 2009.

p. 99 The Meyerson article is found here: https://prospect.org/politics/2024-07-19-party-of-precarious-manhood-trump-dnc/

p. 100 For Hulk Logan's racist rant, see the article by Mya Abraham here: https://www.yahoo.com/news/hulk-hogan-threatens-body-slam-153220260.html?

pp. 100-101 The French article is found here: https://www.nytimes.com/2024/07/28/opinion/hulk-hogan-vance-harris.html

For the Black Madonna, see Fox, *The Hidden Spirituality of Men*, pp. 231-44. See also, Alessandra Belloni, *Healing Journeys with the Black Madonna, Rochester*, Vt: Bear & Co., 2019; and Christena Cleveland, *God is a Black Woman*, NY: HarperOne, 2022.

ACKNOWLEDGEMENTS

I wish to thank Gianluigi Gugliermetto ("GG") for helping to oversee our workshop on Thomas Aquinas in Orvieto and for showing me the frescoes by Signorelli along with his generous assistance in editing this book. And to Claudia Picardi for her assistance with the front cover. Also, Dennis Edwards for his work in sponsoring that workshop and his commitment daily supporting me and the creation spirituality movement.

And thanks to Ron Tuazon for his support and encouragement. To Aaron Stern of the Academy of the Love of Learning and to Lama Tsomo for their friendship and generous enthusiasm and support over the years, a very deep bow and thank you.

I am deeply grateful to Caroline Myss for leading off this book with a substantive reflection from a seasoned teacher on the nature of archetypes. And on such very short notice, I thank you for your generosity. I also thank Andrew Harvey for his challenging, enthusiastic and auspicious Afterward and his deep encouragement while writing this book.

I owe to Nicholas Fox Weber for his brilliant study on *Freud's Trip to Orvieto* which reinforced my own deep experience with the "Antichrist" fresco. I also want to thank Jungian scholar Steve Herrmann for his thoughts on archetypes and alerting me to Edward Edinger's study on the Apocalypse archetype. Of course,

my thanks goes out to all those thinkers and mystics over the centuries whom I cite in the text and footnotes with a special salute here to Aquinas, Hildegard, Eckhart, and Julian of Norwich. Thanks to Melanie Lear and the other managers at i-Universe who have assisted in getting this book into print in a timely fashion for the upcoming election. And to Alan Mayer of Starfish Recording Studio for his professional creation of the audio version of this book. And to you, reader, for daring to look critically at the presence of evil within and among us and the promise of Christ and other spiritual avatars in these perilous and decisive times.
August 15, 2024

Feast of the Assumption (a celebration of the Divine Feminine to balance a healthy Sacred Masculine)

ABOUT THE AUTHOR

Matthew Fox is author of forty-three books on culture and spirituality, which have been translated into seventy-nine languages and received many awards. He graduated from the Institut Catholique de Paris with a doctorate in the history and theology of spiritualities. In his books and teaching and designing of spirituality programs, he has brought alive the much-neglected western tradition of creation spirituality.

He lectures internationally and has created a pedagogy for teaching spirituality that has reached many thousands of persons through Mundelein College in Chicago, Holy Names College, and the University of Creation Spirituality, which he founded and led for nine years in Oakland, California, along with his pilot program, YELLAWE, for inner city youth.

For speaking out on women's rights, gay rights, and Native American rights, he was silenced for a year and later expelled from the Dominican Order under the papacies of John Paul II and Benedict XVI. He then joined the Episcopal Church to work with young people to create a postmodern form of ritual and worship known as the "Cosmic Mass" that incorporates dance, DJ, VJ, rap, and other postmodern art forms. He is cofounder of the Order of the Sacred Earth and, since Mother's Day 2019, has offered free daily meditations at www.dailymeditationswithmatthewfox.org

Fox is a visiting scholar at the Academy for the Love of Learning in Santa Fe, New Mexico, and teaches frequently on the Shift Network. He is a recipient of the Abbey Courage of Conscience Peace Award, whose other recipients include the Dalai Lama, Rosa Parks, Mother Teresa, Ernesto Cardinale, and Maya Angelou. Other awards include the Gandhi, King, Ikeda Community Builder Prize from Morehouse College, the Humanities Award of the Sufi International Association of Sufism, the Tikkun Ethics Award, INTA Humanitarian Award, and the New Thought Walden Award.

About his work, the late Father Bede Griffiths said: Matthew Fox's "creation spirituality is the spirituality of the future, and his theology of the Cosmic Christ is the theology of the future." Father Thomas Berry said: "Matthew Fox might well be the most creative, the most comprehensive, surely the most challenging religious-spiritual thinker that has emerged from within the contemporary Christian tradition in America. He has the scholarship, the imagination, the courage, the writing skill to fulfill this role at a time when the more official Christian theological traditions are having difficulty in establishing any vital contact with either the spiritual possibilities of the present or with their own most creative spiritual traditions of the past." Fox's papers are available by contacting the Boulder, Colorado Libraries' Rare & Distinctive Collections at rad@colorado.edu.

See www.matthewfox.org

BOOKS BY MATTHEW FOX

Original Blessing

The Coming of the Cosmic Christ

A Spirituality Named Compassion

Order of the Sacred Earth: An Intergenerational Vision of Love and Action (with Skylar Wilson and Jennifer Listug)

Julian of Norwich: Wisdom in a Time of Pandemic—and *Beyond*

Prayer: A Radical Response to Life

Creation Spirituality: Liberating Gifts for the Peoples of the Earth

Whee! We, Wee All the Way Home: Toward a Prophetic, Sensual Spirituality

Western Spirituality: Historical Roots, Ecumenical Routes (editor)

Natural Grace (with Rupert Sheldrake)

The Physics of Angels (with Rupert Sheldrake)

Christian Mystics: 365 Readings and Meditations

Passion for Creation: The Earth-Honoring Spirituality of Meister Eckhart:

Meister Eckhart: A Mystic-Warrior for Our Times

Meditations with Meister Eckhart

Illuminations of Hildegard of Bingen

Hildegard of Bingen, A Saint for Our Times: Unleashing Her Power in the 21st Century

Hildegard of Bingen's Book of Divine Works, *Songs and Letters*

Sheer Joy: Conversations with Thomas Aquinas on Creation Spirituality
A Way to God: Thomas Merton's Creation Spirituality Journey
The Reinvention of Work: A New Vision of Livelihood for Our Times
Creativity: Where the Divine and the Human Meet
The Hidden Spirituality of Men: Ten Metaphors to Awaken the Sacred Masculine
The A.W.E Project: Reinventing Education, Reinventing the Human
Occupy Spirituality: A Radical Vision for a New Generation (with Adam Bucko)
Sins of the Spirit, Blessings of the Flesh: Transforming Evil in Soul and Society
Wrestling with the Prophets: Essays on Creations Spirituality and Everyday Life
The Pope's War: Why Ratzinger's Secret Crusade Has Imperiled the Church and What Can Be Saved
Confessions: The Making of a Post-Denominational Priest
One River, Many Wells: Wisdom Springing from Global Faiths
Religion USA: Culture and Religion by way of Time *Magazine*
A New Reformation
Letters to Pope Francis
Naming the Unnameable: 89 Wonderful and Useful Names for God . . . Including the Unnameable God
Stations of the Cosmic Christ (with Bishop Marc Andrus)
The Lotus & the Rose: Dialogs on Buddhism and Christian Mysticism (with Lama Tsomo)
Matthew Fox: Essential Writings on Creation Spirituality (Part of the "Modern Spiritual Masters Series" by Orbis Books)
The Tao of Thomas Aquinas: Fierce Wisdom for Hard Times

To order any of these books, visit matthewfox.org.

Printed in Dunstable, United Kingdom